THE HOLY SPIRIT

A PILGRIMAGE
SMALL GROUP GUIDE BY
MARLENE NATHAN

NAVPRESS
BRINGING TRUTH TO LIFE
P.O. Box 35001, Colorado Springs, Colorado 80935

OUR GUARANTEE TO YOU

We believe so strongly in the message of our books that we are making this quality guarantee to you. If for any reason you are disappointed with the content of this book, return the title page to us with your name and address and we will refund to you the list price of the book. To help us serve you better, please briefly describe why you were disappointed. Mail your refund request to: NavPress, P.O. Box 35002, Colorado Springs, CO 80935.

The Navigators is an international Christian organization. Our mission is to reach, disciple, and equip people to know Christ and to make Him known through successive generations. We envision multitudes of diverse people in the United States and every other nation who have a passionate love for Christ, live a lifestyle of sharing Christ's love, and multiply spiritual laborers among those without Christ.

NavPress is the publishing ministry of The Navigators. NavPress publications help believers learn biblical truth and apply what they learn to their lives and ministries. Our mission is to stimulate spiritual formation among our readers.

2 3 4 5 6 7 8 9 10 11 12 13 14 15 / 09 08 07 06 05 04 03 02 01

FOR A FREE CATALOG OF
NAVPRESS BOOKS & BIBLE STUDIES,
CALL 1-800-366-7788 (USA).
IN CANADA, CALL 1-416-499-4615.

Contents

How This Study Guide Works

Relating to the Holy Spirit

The breath of God. Wind. Fire. Dove. Counselor. Helper. Bringer of truth. Giver of gifts. Source of power. Descriptions like these pique our interest in the Holy Spirit. If we are followers of Christ, then the Holy Spirit lives in us, yet many of us wonder how to relate to Him. Who is He? How does a person live in the power of the Spirit? Cultivate the fruit of the Spirit? Exercise the gifts of the Spirit? Practice the presence of the Spirit? These are the kinds of questions this study will address.

Using a small-group format, participants will:

► engage in individual and group reflection
► participate in creative Bible study
► learn to receive care from other group members
► pray together for the Holy Spirit's work in each person's life

Building Community

The life of following Christ was never meant to be solitary. The early Christians pursued it in groups not much larger than your small group. They met exclusively in homes for the first two hundred years or so of the movement. By meeting in a small group, you are imitating a time-tested format for spiritual life.

People join small groups for all sorts of reasons: to get to know a few people well, to be cared for, to learn, to grow spiritually. We believe small groups are the ideal setting in which people can both learn what it means to take on the character of Christ and also practice the process of becoming like Christ. While there are many spiritually helpful things one can do alone or in a large group, a small group offers many advantages. Among other things, group members can:

- ► encourage one another in good times and bad
- ► ask thoughtful questions when a member has a decision to make
- ► listen to God together
- ► learn how to pray for each other
- ► benefit from one another's insights into the Scriptures
- ► acquire a habit of reading the Bible on a regular basis
- ► practice loving their neighbors
- ► worship God together
- ► learn to communicate effectively
- ► solve problems together
- ► learn to receive care from others
- ► experience the pleasure of helping another person grow

This Growth Guide emphasizes learning and practice. It will help you get to know the Holy Spirit in a non-threatening group environment. You will engage in reflection, study, interaction, and prayer. You will be challenged to put into practice what you are learning during the week.

A Modular Approach

Each session is divided into ten modules or sections. Suggested times are allocated among the modules so that you can complete the session in 60 to 90 minutes. The modules are:

Overview: The first page of each session briefly describes the objectives for your meeting so that you will know what to expect during the meeting and what results to strive for. You will also learn something about the author's own story as it relates to the topic at hand.

Beginning: Building relationships is a necessary part of each group experience. Each session will have several questions to help you learn who the other members are and where they have been in their lives. The beginning questions also help you begin thinking about a particular issue in preparation for your time of Bible study and problem solving.

The Text: Studying a biblical text is an integral part of this guide. You will examine brief passages from various parts of the Bible. THE MESSAGE by Eugene Peterson and the NEW INTERNATIONAL VERSION have been chosen where appropriate. THE

MESSAGE is deliberately relational and will help those familiar with Scripture to see certain passages with new eyes. Since the New Testament was written to be read aloud, you will begin your study by reading the text aloud. Words in bold type are explained in the Reference Notes section.

Understanding the Text: Unless you notice carefully what the text says, you will not be able to interpret it accurately. The questions in this section will help you focus on the key issues and wrestle with what the text means. In this section you will concentrate on the passage in its original first-century context.

Applying the Text: It is not enough to simply understand the passage; you need to apply that understanding to your situation. The questions in this section connect what you have read to how you intend to live.

Assignment: To allow for flexibility between group and individual learning, this guide offers homework as an elective. Your group may discuss the options found in each session as a possible means of continued growth and reflection. Make sure that every group member agrees to do work before assigning it.

Prayer: Praying together can be one of the most faith-and relationship-building things you do together. Suggestions are made to facilitate this time in the group.

Reference Notes: In order to accurately understand the meaning of the text, one needs to know a little about the context in which it was written and the key words and phrases it contains. The notes include background on the characters, information about cultural practices, word definitions, and so on. You will find entries in this section for those words and phrases in the text that are printed in bold type. You can scan the notes after reading the text aloud or during your discussion of Understanding the Text.

Additional Resources: A list of books that address the session topics is on pages 111-112.

Help for the Leader

This Growth Guide provides everything the leader needs to facilitate the group's discussion. In each session, the symbol ❶ designates instructions for the leader.

Answers to Common Questions

Who is this material designed for?

- ► Anyone who wants to learn about the Holy Spirit.
- ► Ongoing groups that want to see the Holy Spirit become more active in their midst.

How often should we meet?

- ► Once a week is best; every other week works as well.

How long should we meet?

- ► You will need at least an hour.
- ► Ninety minutes is best—this gives time for more discussion.
- ► Some groups may want to meet for two hours, especially if you have more than eight people.

What if we only have 50 minutes?

- ► Cut back on the Beginning section and choose just one question under Applying the Text. Pray only briefly.

Is homework necessary?

- ► No, the group can meet with no prior preparation.
- ► The assignments will greatly increase what you gain from the group.

Another Counselor: Introducing the Holy Spirit

John 14:15-18,25-27; 16:5-15

God the Creator, the God who had come alongside men in Jesus, now made himself available to come within their very personalities. It is inconceivable that anyone sat down to think out any doctrine so intrinsically improbable as the Trinity.[1]

Our understanding of God is forever marked by the fact that in Christ he has been "fleshed out" at one point in our human history. . . . We must recognize the same to be true about the Spirit, not simply theoretically but really and experientially. The Spirit is not lightly called the Spirit of Jesus Christ. Christ has put a human face on the Spirit as well.[2]

Overview

❶ *Have someone read aloud this introduction.*

Perhaps the most confusing Person of the Trinity for me has been the Holy Spirit. I prefer relating to God the Father and God the Son because "father" and "son" are concepts I am familiar with. But God the Holy Spirit has been a mystery to me for much of my Christian life. There is nothing or no one anywhere in my experience quite like Him. If I try to imagine Him, the best I can come up with is an image like the "Force" from the *Star Wars* movies.

My problem is that the Holy Spirit is intangible. I cannot touch Him with my hands, see Him with my eyes, or hear Him with my ears. I can't even picture in my mind what He might be like. Yet throughout Scripture He is said to "fill" people (Exodus 31:3, Acts 2:4), "come on" people (Judges 3:10, Ezekiel 11:5), "speak" through people (2 Samuel 23:2), even "move" people (Isaiah 34:16, Ezekiel 3:14). Add to this all the many unusual and sometimes bizarre things believers have attributed to the Holy Spirit over the centuries, and it's no wonder some of us would feel more comfortable if His presence were limited to the biblical passages describing His work.

What has helped me to both understand and embrace the Holy Spirit is that Jesus of Nazareth, the God-man (and my trusted Friend), had much to say about Him. During His three years of ministry, Jesus spoke often of the Father. But as His earthly ministry was coming to a close, He began to speak more and more about the Spirit. Jesus told His disciples, "Anyone who has seen me has seen the Father" (John 14:9). The same could almost be said of the Holy Spirit. As Gordon Fee writes, "Christ has put a human face on the Spirit as well."[3]

On the night before His death, Jesus began to prepare His disciples for the coming of the Holy Spirit. In just a little over fifty days, they would be meeting the Spirit in person! In this study of John 14 and 16, we will discover what Jesus told His disciples about the Spirit and consider how these truths apply to our relationship with the Holy Spirit today.

▼ ▼ ▼ ▼ ▼ ▼ ▼ ▼ ▼ ▼ ▼ ▼ ▼ ▼ ▼ ▼ ▼ ▼
Beginning   15 minutes

❶ *These sharing questions at the beginning of the session are intended to help the group get to know each other. They will draw out the assumptions and questions each person brings to the study. Allow each person to answer the first question before moving to the next one. As leader, you should be the first to answer each beginning question. In later sections you will not be the first to answer.*

1. When you think of the Holy Spirit, what picture, idea, or feeling comes to mind?

2. What is one question you hope this study of the Holy Spirit will answer? (If you have more than one question, you can list them.)

❶ *Write down everyone's questions about the Spirit, so you can check the list week by week to see whether the questions are being addressed.*

The Text   5 minutes

❶ *Using the reference notes on "setting" (page 17), set the scene for the group. Help people imagine the disciples' state of mind. Then have someone read the text aloud. You may also want to refer the group to the other reference notes.*

"If you love me, you will obey what I command. And I will ask the Father, and he will give you **another Counselor** to be with you forever—the Spirit of truth. The world cannot accept him, because it neither sees him nor knows him. But you know him, for he lives with you and will be in you. I will not leave you as orphans; I will come to you. . . .

"All this I have spoken while still with you. But the Counselor, the Holy Spirit, **whom the Father will send** in my name, will teach you all things and will remind you of everything I have said to you. Peace I leave with you; my peace I give you. I do not give to you as the world gives. Do not let your hearts be troubled and do not be afraid." (John 14:15-18,25-27)

"Now I am going to him who sent me, yet none of you asks me, 'Where are you going?' Because I have said these things, you are filled with grief. But I tell you the truth: It is for your good that I am going away. **Unless I go away, the Counselor will not come** to you; but if I go, **I will send him** to you. When he comes, he will **convict** the world of guilt in regard to **sin** and **righteousness** and **judgment**: in regard to sin, because men do not believe in me; in regard to righteousness, because I am going to the Father, where you can see me no longer; in regard to judgment, because the prince of this world now stands condemned.

"I have much more to say to you, more than you can now bear. But when he, the Spirit of truth, comes, he will guide you into all truth. He will not speak on his own; he will speak only what he hears, and he will tell you what is yet to come. He will bring glory to me by taking from what is mine and making it known to you. All that belongs to the Father is mine. That is why I said the Spirit will take from what is mine and make it known to you."

(John 16:5-15)

▼ ▼ ▼ ▼ ▼ ▼ ▼ ▼ ▼ ▼ ▼ ▼ ▼ ▼ ▼ ▼ ▼ ▼

Understanding the Text   20 minutes

3. a. List all the specific things Jesus says in this passage about the Spirit.

   b. Which of these are also true of Jesus? (You can compare Matthew 28:20; John 1:10; John 7:16,28-29; 14:6.) Which things are unique to the Spirit?

4. According to Jesus, if we love Him, then we'll obey Him. What does this mean? What does it *not* mean?

5. Jesus consistently refers to the Holy Spirit as "He," not "It." What does that tell you about the Spirit? What are some characteristics that are true of people that are not true of things?

6. Jesus refers to the Holy Spirit as "another Counselor." How would you explain in your own words what this title means? (You might review the notes on page 19.)

7. a. Jesus assures the disciples that they will not be abandoned like "orphans" but that He will come to them. What different comings might Jesus be referring to?

   b. What is special about the coming of the Spirit?

8. a. Jesus says the world cannot accept the Holy Spirit. Why not?

   b. How do you reconcile this statement with Jesus' earlier words that God loves the world and sent Christ to save it (John 3:16-17)?

9. The disciples are understandably distressed to hear that Jesus plans to leave them. What does He say to encourage them in their grief?

10. What does it mean for the Spirit to "convict the world of guilt . . . (you may want to see the reference notes on pages 17-19).

in regard to sin"?

in regard to righteousness"?

in regard to judgment"?

Applying the Text   20 minutes

11. a. Jesus said that love for Him and obedience to His Word are necessary prerequisites for experiencing the Holy Spirit. What thoughts go through your mind when you read a sentence like, "If you love me, you will obey what I command"?

❑ I'm a failure at that. Why try?
❑ I don't like all this talk about obedience, as though Christ is a demanding boss.

❏ I do try to obey Christ, but I often feel inadequate.
❏ I know my obedience isn't perfect, but I also know I genuinely love Christ.
❏ Other:

b. In your own words, how do you think Jesus wants you to respond to His statement?

12. Jesus says His disciples know the Spirit, for the Spirit lives *with* them and will be *in* them. How do you think this statement should affect your relationship with the Holy Spirit?

13. Describe how the Holy Spirit has done any of the following:

❏ taught you about spiritual things

❏ reminded you of what Jesus said

❏ guided you into truth

❏ connected you with Jesus and the Father

❏ been a counselor, a comforter, and a helper who is like Jesus to you

Jesus made the Holy Spirit sound rather self-effacing—the Spirit speaks only what He hears, and He brings glory to Jesus. Many Christians believe that the Holy Spirit would never do anything that would draw attention to Himself. His role is to exalt Jesus. Yet Jesus said the same things about Himself: He spoke and did only what the Father told Him, and He sought to glorify the Father (John 5:30; 7:16; 8:50; 12:28).

14. In our next session we'll see that when the Spirit was first given, He attracted a lot of attention, and some of it was to Himself (see Acts 2:17-21). How do you think we ought to strike the right balance between over-emphasizing and under-emphasizing the Holy Spirit?

15. What have you learned about the Holy Spirit through this discussion that you didn't fully understand before?

Assignment   5 minutes

Make a list of all the truths about the Holy Spirit you discovered through this session. Then make another list of all the questions you still have about the Spirit. As you progress through this guide, refer back to these lists to see if your questions are being answered and to add new truths as you learn them.

Prayer   5 minutes

Offer thanksgiving to God for all the different blessings that come to you through the Holy Spirit. Pray for each other that the Holy Spirit would increasingly take what belongs to Jesus and make it known to you (John 16:15).

▼ ▼ ▼ ▼ ▼ ▼ ▼ ▼ ▼ ▼ ▼ ▼ ▼ ▼ ▼ ▼ ▼ ▼ ▼ ▼

Reference Notes

Setting: The disciples are celebrating the Passover alone with Jesus. Jesus has been teaching them through actions: He has washed their feet, setting an example of humility and service (John 13:1-17). He has also used the bread and wine of the meal to illustrate the meaning of His coming death (Luke 22:14-20, 1 Corinthians 11:23-26). Now He is teaching through words. He tells His disciples that He is about to leave, and they cannot go with Him. These men have left everything, burning their bridges behind them, in order to follow Jesus, and now He's leaving!? They are distressed. What trouble is coming? How will they handle it all alone? So Jesus comforts them and tells them not to be troubled (John 14:1). But they already are! He goes on to promise the following:

► "You are guaranteed heaven." (14:1-2)
► "I will come back for you." (14:3)
► "Your ultimate destination is the Father and I am the only way you will make it there." (14:4-7)
► "I and the Father are uniquely one." (14:8-10)
► "You will soon be following in my footsteps and doing the things I have been doing." (14:12-14)

This last promise leads right into the discussion about the Spirit. If the disciples are going to do what Jesus did, then they will need power!

If you love me: Jesus is not suggesting here that everything we receive from God (His love, the Holy Spirit) is contingent upon our ability to love Him. He is saying that love precedes obedience and that real love reveals itself in actions. Neither is Jesus suggesting that loving God is the price tag for receiving the Holy Spirit. Rather, He is laying out the relational context for the giving of the Spirit.

another: Jesus calls the Spirit *another* Counselor. The Greek word *allon* implies "another of the same kind," not another that is perhaps different. The disciples have had one parakleton: Jesus. Now they will have another.

17

Counselor: Different English words have been used to translate this Greek word *parakleton*, such as counselor, comforter, advocate, and helper. The word literally means one who is called alongside to encourage and exhort. In secular writing, it was usually used to refer to legal assistance in a court of law. The word is used of Jesus in this sense in 1 John 2:1. Most theologians believe the Spirit's work has such legal overtones but that His work goes beyond that.

whom the Father will send . . . I will send him: Throughout his Gospel, John seems to confuse the Father, Jesus, and the Spirit. He says that the Father will send the Spirit, then that Jesus will do so. He says the Spirit will be in us, then that Jesus will be in us. But John is not confused, nor is he contradicting himself. This is John's way of describing the close interrelationship and unity between God the Father, God the Son, and God the Holy Spirit.

Unless I go away, the Counselor will not come: Jesus is not suggesting here that He and the Spirit cannot be in the same place at the same time, nor that He must first leave before the Spirit will come to replace Him. Jesus may be referring to His going to the cross. If He does not die for the sin of the world, the Spirit will never be sent. Or, He may be saying that His work of redemption needs to be complete (including His ascension to the Father, John 7:39) before the Spirit will come.

convict: The Greek word *elencho* has a broad meaning and is translated over ten different ways throughout the New Testament. Here, it seems to mean (1) to prove guilty and (2) to awaken a consciousness of that guilt. The gospel proves that the entire world is guilty (Romans 1–3), but the Holy Spirit makes that guilt real and personal (Acts 2:37). With believers, the Spirit is like a defense attorney (an advocate), but with the world, He is like the prosecutor!

sin: The Holy Spirit could convict everyone, believers and unbelievers alike, of sin because everyone is a sinner. The unique sin of the world is that they reject Christ (John 3:18, 15:22).

righteousness: The world has the wrong standards for righteousness. People believed that they were righteous in killing Jesus, that He was the sinner and deserved to die (Matthew 27:39-44). By going to the Father and leaving behind an empty tomb, Jesus proved His own righteousness and approval by the

18

Father. Only the Spirit can convince the world (corporately and individually) of this truth.

judgment: The Cross brought about Satan's defeat (Colossians 2:13-15), which was a form of judgment against him. His final demise is yet to come, however, and he is still at work in those who do not believe (Ephesians 2:1-2). As certain as his judgment was and ultimately will be, so is the judgment that awaits all those in the world who refuse to believe. The Holy Spirit alone is able to convince the unbeliever of the reality and certainty of future judgment.

---

1. Michael Green, *I Believe in the Holy Spirit* (Grand Rapids: Eerdmans, 1975), p. 16.
2. Gordon D. Fee, *Paul, the Spirit and the People of God* (Peabody, Mass.: Hendrickson, 1996), p. 25.
3. Fee, p. 25.

Clothed with Power: The Spirit is Given

Acts 2:1-24,32-33,36-39

Imagine visiting a town at night that appears to have no lights, no televisions—not even alarm clocks. And then imagine learning that the town's power supply is virtually infinite, but that no one in the town had thought to turn any of their electrical appliances on. Wouldn't that town seem like a silly place to you? Yet the Church is all too often like that town. God has given us the power of His Spirit to fulfill His mission in the world, yet few Christians have even begun to depend on His power.[1]

▼ ▼ ▼ ▼ ▼ ▼ ▼ ▼ ▼ ▼ ▼ ▼ ▼ ▼ ▼ ▼ ▼ ▼

Overview   5 minutes

❶ *Ask someone to recap what you learned from session 1. Then ask someone to read aloud the following.*

According to Webster's Dictionary, an experience is "something personally encountered, undergone, or lived through." Throughout church history, people have had experiences with God that have profoundly affected their lives and subsequent ministries. On May 24th, 1738, on Aldersgate Street in London, John Wesley said, "I felt my heart strangely warmed" as he listened to a reading of Luther's commentary on Romans.[2] Upon the death of

Blaise Pascal, the famous French philosopher and mathematician, the following was found written on a bit of paper sewn into his shirt:

> This day of Grace 1654: From about half past ten at night, to about half after midnight, Fire. Fire. God of Abraham, God of Isaac, God of Jacob, not of the philosophers and the wise . . . God of Jesus Christ. . . . O Righteous Father, the world hath not known Thee, but I have known Thee. Joy, joy, joy, tears of joy.[3]

Dwight L. Moody, the greatest evangelist of the nineteenth century had this experience:

> Well, one day in the city of New York, oh what a day, I cannot describe it. I seldom refer to it. It is almost too sacred an experience to name. Paul had an experience of which he never spoke for fourteen years, I can only say that God revealed himself to me and I had such an experience of his love and presence that I had to ask him to stay his hand.[4]

Whenever we have an experience with God, we are encountering the Holy Spirit. I once experienced the Holy Spirit when I was mowing our lawn. I had just graduated from high school and was about to go off to college. I had been a Christian about two years but thought sharing the gospel message with others was optional. While I was using a power mower and not thinking about anything in particular, God began to speak to me. He didn't speak with an audible voice, but I could hear the words clearly in my mind. It was as though the sound of the mower was drowned out by these words. I knew without any doubt that it was God.

I finished mowing the lawn, got on my bike, and rode around the neighborhood. God was telling me that He loved all the people in the houses I was riding by and that I *needed* to tell them so. I *must* share the gospel message so people would know how much God loved them. This went on for about two hours. When it was over, my heart was changed. Now I *wanted* to evangelize. I believe I experienced what Paul describes as Christ's love compelling us (2 Corinthians 5:14). I went off to college that fall committed to evangelizing my fellow students.

Throughout the Old and New Testaments, people's experiences with God are recorded so that today believers can learn and benefit from them. In this study of Acts 2 we will examine what happened when the Holy Spirit was first given, why it happened, and what the results were. Then we will consider what the implications of this first Pentecost are for believers today.

▼ ▼ ▼ ▼ ▼ ▼ ▼ ▼ ▼ ▼ ▼ ▼ ▼ ▼ ▼ ▼ ▼ ▼ ▼ ▼

Beginning   10 minutes

❶ *Allow each person to answer the first question before moving to the next one. The leader should answer first each time.*

1. Not all experiences with God are as dramatic as what Pascal and Moody described. Share an experience you've had that you believe is from the Holy Spirit, such as:

   ❏ "Hearing" God speak to you personally through His Word
   ❏ Being convicted of a particular sin
   ❏ Feeling led to take a certain course of action
   ❏ Insight about another person that doesn't seem like mere intuition
   ❏ A prophetic word or message
   ❏ Other:

2. What effect did this experience have in your life?

▼ ▼ ▼ ▼ ▼ ▼ ▼ ▼ ▼ ▼ ▼ ▼ ▼ ▼ ▼ ▼ ▼ ▼ ▼

The Text   5 minutes

Jesus had promised several times that the Holy Spirit would come upon His followers with power. That promise was fulfilled at the Jewish feast of Pentecost.

❶ *Have someone read the text aloud. You may also read some or all of the reference notes on pages 30-32.*

When the day of **Pentecost** came, they were all together in one place. Suddenly a sound like the blowing of a violent **wind** came from heaven and filled the whole house where they were sitting. They saw what seemed to be **tongues** of **fire** that separated and came to rest on each of them. All of them were **filled with the Holy Spirit** and began to speak in other **tongues** as the Spirit enabled them.

Now there were staying in Jerusalem God-fearing Jews from every nation under heaven. When they heard this sound, a crowd came together in bewilderment, because each one heard them speaking in his own language. Utterly amazed, they asked: "Are not all these men who are speaking **Galileans**? Then how is it that each of us hears them in his own native language? **Parthians**, **Medes** and Elamites; residents of Mesopotamia, Judea and Cappadocia, Pontus and Asia, Phrygia and Pamphylia, Egypt and the parts of Libya near Cyrene; visitors from Rome (both Jews and converts to Judaism); Cretans and Arabs—we hear them declaring the wonders of God in our own tongues!" Amazed and perplexed, they asked one another, "What does this mean?"

Some, however, made fun of them and said, "They have had too much wine."

Then Peter stood up with the Eleven, raised his voice and **addressed** the crowd: "Fellow Jews and all of you who live in Jerusalem, let me explain this to you; listen carefully to what I say. These men are not drunk, as you suppose. It's only nine in the morning! No, this is what was spoken by the prophet Joel:

"'In **the last days**, God says,
I will pour out my Spirit on all people.
Your sons and daughters will prophesy,
your young men will see visions,

24

your old men will dream dreams.
Even on my servants, both men and women,
I will pour out my Spirit in those days,
and they will prophesy.
I will show wonders in the heaven above
and signs on the earth below,
blood and fire and billows of smoke.
The sun will be turned to darkness
and the moon to blood
before the coming of **the great and glorious day of the
Lord.**
And everyone who calls
on the name of the Lord will be saved.'

"Men of Israel, listen to this: Jesus of Nazareth was a man
accredited by God to you by miracles, wonders and signs, which
God did among you through him, as you yourselves know. This
man was handed over to you by God's set purpose and fore-
knowledge; and you, with the help of wicked men, put him to
death by nailing him to the cross. But God raised him from the
dead, freeing him from the agony of death, because it was
impossible for death to keep its hold on him. . . . God has raised
this Jesus to life, and we are all witnesses of the fact. Exalted to
the right hand of God, he has received from the Father the
promised Holy Spirit and has poured out what you now see and
hear. . . .
    "Therefore let all Israel be assured of this: God has made
this Jesus, whom you crucified, both Lord and Christ."
    When the people heard this, they were cut to the heart and
said to Peter and the other apostles, "Brothers, what shall we do?"
    Peter replied, "Repent and be baptized, every one of you, **in
the name of Jesus Christ** for the forgiveness of your sins. And
you will receive the gift of the Holy Spirit. The promise is for
you and your children and for all who are far off—for all whom
the Lord our God will call."
    . . . Those who accepted his message were baptized, and
about **three thousand** were added to their number that day.

(Acts 2:1-24,32-33,36-39,41)

Understanding the Text   20 minutes

3. The disciples were probably in the temple courts on
   Pentecost, so this would not have been a private meeting.
   What specific things happened at this meeting, according to
   the first paragraph of the text?

4. a. What did the Spirit enable the disciples to do?

   b. What purpose did this serve?

5. Although everyone in the temple was witnessing a miracle
   from God (Galileans speaking so many different languages),
   why do you think they had such different responses?

6. Just fifty-one days earlier, Peter had behaved like a coward,
   denying he even knew Jesus to a servant girl (Luke 22:56-
   57). After the resurrection, Peter still seemed defeated and
   decided to go fishing, something he had once given up to
   follow Christ (see John 21:3). Now he boldly stood up to
   offer an explanation to the crowd. What does this tell you

about the depth of change that being "filled with the Holy Spirit" can bring?

7. Before preaching the gospel message, Peter took time to respond to the crowd's "bewilderment." How did he explain the unusual phenomenon?

8. Peter then declared the message that was to become the core of the movement's faith: "Jesus of Nazareth was a man accredited by God . . . you put him to death. . . . But God raised him from the dead . . . and we are all witnesses of the fact." What role do you think the Holy Spirit played in the formation and presentation of this message?

9. The crowd was "cut to the heart" and appealed to Peter as to what they should do next. Jesus had said that part of the Holy Spirit's job would be to convict the world of guilt (John 16:8). In this situation, what had the Spirit done to convict the crowd?

10. Peter gave the crowd specific instructions about what they should do in response to his message. Then he told them that they *and* their children *and* people "who are far off" could receive the gift of the Holy Spirit, just as the disciples had. Do you think Peter is referring to the same kind of power that was displayed throughout Acts 2? What leads you to that conclusion?

Applying the Text   20 minutes

11. Imagine yourself as one of the disciples when the room filled with the sound of the wind, tongues of fire seemed to appear over people's heads, and you all started speaking in foreign languages. Jesus had not told you what to expect when the Spirit was given, although powerful phenomena often occurred in the Old Testament when people were filled with the Spirit. How do you think you would have felt during this experience?

12. Christians today debate whether the Holy Spirit still does extra-ordinary things like these, or whether the events recorded in Acts were unique to the founding of the church. On what do you think we should base our opinions about this?

13. What do you expect should normally happen today when people "receive the gift of the Holy Spirit"?

14. Peter was a changed man because of the pouring out of the Spirit on that Pentecost. Some of the event's effects were constant. On the other hand, Peter was "filled with the Holy Spirit" periodically when the need arose. (See Acts 4:8, as well as reference note on page 30.) What sort of changes do you think being filled with the Spirit would bring (or have brought) in your life?

15. Is there a connection between the filling of the Holy Spirit and evangelism today? How should this connection, or lack of connection, affect the way the people of God go about the work of God in the world?

Assignment

Write down in your own words how you would share the gospel message with someone. Make sure you include the essential facts of the message, plus some of your own experience of the resurrected Christ. Practice saying what you wrote, concentrating on being natural and clear in your communication style.

Pray privately for specific people you know and/or situations in your life where the gospel is needed. Keep a journal to record what God does!

Prayer   5 minutes

Pray for each other to be clothed with the power of the Holy Spirit for evangelism. Believe God and take Him at His Word that the promise is to you "who are far off." If you feel comfortable, lay hands on each person individually, praying specifically for that person, his or her needs, and his or her opportunities for sharing the message. Be sure to *wait* long enough for the Holy Spirit to work in each person.

Reference Notes

Setting: The Gospel of Luke and the book of Acts are companion volumes of history. They were both written by Luke, the beloved physician and traveling companion of the apostle Paul.

Jesus had instructed His disciples that before they were to do *anything*, they must wait in Jerusalem to be "clothed with power" (Luke 24:49) and "baptized with the Holy Spirit" (Acts 1:5). This experience would enable His followers to be witnesses in both word and deed, just as Jesus was (see Acts 5:12-16; 8:4-8). He did not, however, describe this experience in any detail. In Acts 1:9-11, the disciples watched Jesus depart from earth physically and leave them all alone. But as He had promised them, they were not abandoned as orphans. Another Counselor was on the way.

Pentecost: This holiday is called the Feast of Weeks in the Old Testament because it is celebrated seven weeks (fifty days) after Passover. *Pentecost* is Greek for "fiftieth day." It is also known as the "Feast of the Harvest" and the "Day of First Fruits" (Exodus 23:16; 34:22; Leviticus 23:15-21; Numbers 28:26-31; Deuteronomy 16:9-12). It was a joyous festival that celebrated God's blessing on the harvest. Later, Pentecost came to be considered the anniversary of the giving of the Law at Mount Sinai. Jews were supposed to make a pilgrimage to Jerusalem to celebrate Pentecost.

wind: Both in the Hebrew (ruah) and in the Greek (pneuma), the word for breath or wind is the same as the word for spirit. Jesus compared the activity of the Spirit to the wind (John 3:8). The Old Testament often portrayed God as the controlling force behind the wind. In 1 Kings 8:10-11, the temple was filled with the glory (presence) of God.

fire: In the Old Testament, fire signified the presence of God (see Exodus 3:2; 13:21-22; 19:18; Deuteronomy 4:11; Ezekiel 1:4-13). It was an essential part of worship, with altars of incense and burnt offerings. John the Baptist predicted that the coming of the Spirit would be associated with fire (Luke 3:16).

filled with the Holy Spirit: This phrase is used in several different ways in the New Testament to describe the work of the

Spirit. Here, and in Acts 9:17 and Luke 1:15, it refers to an initial endowment. It also describes a subsequent filling that produces speech empowered by the Spirit (Acts 4:8,31; 13:9). In Acts 13:52 and Ephesians 5:18, "filled with the Spirit" refers to an ongoing process. Luke 4:1 and Acts 6:3,5; 7:55; 11:24 refer to the state of being full of the Spirit. The New Testament also uses different words to describe being filled with the Holy Spirit: "baptized" in Acts 1:5 and 11:16; "poured out" in Acts 2:17; and "received" in Acts 10:47.

tongues: Speaking in tongues is listed in 1 Corinthians 12 as a spiritual gift or *charisma,* "a concrete expression of grace." According to 1 Corinthians 14, this gift is Spirit-inspired, yet the speaker remains in control of himself or herself at all times. The speech referred to in 1 Corinthians is apparently unintelligible to both speaker and hearer, so for public use it needs to be interpreted. For private use, however, no interpretation is necessary. The person who speaks in tongues "utters mysteries with his spirit," "speaks . . . to God," and "edifies himself," even though his "mind is unfruitful." In Acts, however, the disciples speak in known languages and no interpretation is necessary. This does not seem to be the norm in the New Testament.[5]

Galileans: People from Galilee were not known to be well-educated, and they spoke with a distinct accent (see Matthew 26:73).

Parthians, Medes: Jews from all over the known world had traveled to Jerusalem for Pentecost. Wars in earlier centuries had driven Jews out of Palestine, and now there were Jewish communities throughout the Middle East. As Jesus promised in Acts 1:8, these pilgrims would now return to their home countries with news of the Messiah.

addressed: The Greek word used here suggests a divinely inspired utterance.

the last days: The New Testament refers to the time between the two comings of Christ as the last days. This is a period where the Kingdom of God has broken into the Kingdom of this world (Luke 11:20), a time when the age to come has overlapped this present age.

the great and glorious day of the Lord: In the Bible, the day of the Lord always meant the day of final judgment where the righteous would be saved and the wicked would be punished. It was associated with cataclysmic events, and most people did not look forward to it. Joel called it "the great and *dreadful* day of the Lord" (Joel 2:31, emphasis added).

in the name of Jesus Christ: Peter is not reciting a liturgical formula here, but emphasizing that when one is baptized, one is personally committed to and identified with the Lord Jesus.

three thousand: It may seem that Luke inflated this number, but it is likely that Jerusalem was swollen with out-of-town Jewish pilgrims. Travel on the sea was dangerous at certain times of the year because of bad weather. Therefore, out of the three annual holy days (Passover, Feast of Booths, and Pentecost), Pentecost would have been the best attended.

---

1. Craig Keener, "Spirit at Work," *Discipleship Journal*, (Jan./Feb. 1996), p. 43.
2. Martin Lloyd-Jones, *Joy Unspeakable: Power and Renewal in the Holy Spirit* (Wheaton, Ill.: Harold Shaw Publishers, 1984), p. 62.
3. Lloyd-Jones, p. 106.
4. Lloyd-Jones, p. 80.
5. For a thorough discussion of tongues, see *Dictionary of Pentecostal and Charismatic Movements*, edited by Stanley M. Burgess, Gary B. McGee & Patrick H. Alexander (Regency Reference Library, Zondervan, 1988), pp. 335-341.

Demonstrations of Power: Jesus and the Spirit

Luke 3:21-23; 4:14-30

Jesus Christ obtained power for His divine works not by His inherent divinity, but by His anointing through the Holy Spirit. He was subject to the same conditions of power as other men.[1]

> *Now wherever the Spirit of God is revealed in the biblical sphere, this happens in a twofold way, en ergo kai logo [in deed and word]. The two belong indissolubly together. The word is never without its accompanying deed and the deed is never without the word that proclaims it. So too with Jesus: the concluding revelation is manifested by acts of power and in words of authority.[2]*

▼ ▼ ▼ ▼ ▼ ▼ ▼ ▼ ▼ ▼ ▼ ▼ ▼ ▼ ▼ ▼ ▼ ▼

Overview   10 minutes

❶ *Ask whether anyone was aware of the Holy Spirit's activity during the week. Let anyone who wishes to do so share briefly about his awareness or lack of awareness of the Spirit. Then ask someone to read aloud the following.*

My favorite part of the school day when I was in kindergarten was show-and-tell. I always liked watching my classmates demonstrate their newest toys and listening to them explain how they worked. I still like show-and-tell today. I'd much prefer to attend a cooking class where I could watch exotic foods actually being prepared than just listen to someone talk.

Jesus' public ministry was a lot like show-and-tell. He both taught and performed miracles. It wouldn't have been enough for Him to do one or the other. This is why some have called Jesus the "Word-Worker." He spoke the words of God, and He did the works of God. In fact, He advised His disciples not to believe the words He said unless He also did the works of the Father (John 14:10-11). And when emissaries from John the Baptist inquired whether or not Jesus was "the one," Jesus responded, "Go back and report to John what you have *seen and heard*" (Luke 7:22, emphasis added).

Show-and-tell is one of the most effective methods of communication. Educators know that the more senses we use in the learning process, the more information we will retain. A student who not only hears a lecture but also watches a demonstration and participates in an experiment will be more likely to remember that lesson. It's one thing to listen to Jesus preach the good news of the kingdom of God. It's quite another to see Him cast a demon out of someone or heal a man born blind. To be able to see the effects of God's kingdom rule played out in a life is powerful. These signs were evidence that the kingdom had in fact come. Jesus was not just all talk. "But if I drive out demons by the finger of God, then the kingdom of God has come to you" (Luke 11:20).

In the past two sessions we have looked at what Jesus taught on the night before His death and the giving of the Spirit seven weeks thereafter. In this session we will flash back three years earlier to examine the beginning of Jesus' public ministry in Luke 3-4. We will learn about His methods of show-and-tell and determine what role the Holy Spirit played in the things Jesus taught and did. In particular, we will focus on the Spirit's role in Jesus' power and authority.

Beginning 10 minutes

Power is the ability to do something. *Authority* is the right to do something. For example, you have the *power* to stop your car when you step on the brake, whereas a policeman has the *authority* to stop your car by raising his hand.

❶ *Let everyone answer the first question before going on to the second. You should answer first each time.*

1. What is something else you have the power to do? Do you use that power?

2. What is something you have authority to do? Do you use it?

The Text 5 minutes

In becoming a human baby, Christ "emptied himself" (Philippians 2:7, NASB) of His divine privileges without ceasing to be God. When He began His ministry, He did so not by His own power and authority, but by the authority of the Father and in the power of the Spirit. The results astonished the Galilean villagers among whom He had grown up.

❶ *Ask someone to read aloud the text. You may also want to read some or all of the reference notes on pages 41-42.*

The people were waiting expectantly and were all wondering in their hearts if **John** might possibly be the Christ. John answered them all, "I baptize you with water. But one more powerful than I will come, the thongs of whose sandals I am not worthy to

untie. He will baptize you with the **Holy Spirit** and with fire . . . "
(Luke 3:15-16).

When all the people were being baptized, **Jesus was baptized too**. And as he was praying, heaven was opened and the Holy Spirit descended on him in bodily form like a **dove**. And a voice came from heaven: "You are my Son, whom I love; with you I am well pleased."

Now Jesus himself was about thirty years old when he began his ministry (Luke 3:21-23).

Jesus returned to Galilee in the **power** of the Spirit, and news about him spread through the whole countryside. He taught in their synagogues, and everyone praised him.

He went to Nazareth, where he had been brought up, and on the Sabbath day he went into the **synagogue,** as was his custom. And he stood up to read. The scroll of the prophet Isaiah was handed to him. Unrolling it, he found the place where it is written:

> "The Spirit of the Lord is on me,
> because he has **anointed** me
> to preach good news to the poor.
> He has sent me to proclaim freedom for the prisoners
> and recovery of sight for the blind,
> to release the oppressed,
> to proclaim the year of the Lord's favor."

Then he rolled up the scroll, gave it back to the attendant and sat down. The eyes of everyone in the synagogue were fastened on him, and he began by saying to them, "Today this scripture is fulfilled in your hearing."

All spoke well of him and were amazed at the gracious words that came from his lips. "Isn't this Joseph's son?" they asked.

Jesus said to them, "Surely you will quote this proverb to me: 'Physician, heal yourself! Do here in your hometown what we have heard that you did in Capernaum.'"

"I tell you the truth," he continued, "no prophet is accepted in his hometown. I assure you that there were many widows in Israel in Elijah's time, when the sky was shut for three and a half years and there was a severe famine throughout the land. Yet Elijah was not sent to any of them, but to a **widow in Zarephath** in the region of Sidon. And there were many in Israel with leprosy in the time of Elisha the prophet, yet not one of them was cleansed—only **Naaman the Syrian**."

All the people in the synagogue were furious when they heard this. They got up, drove him out of the town, and took him to the brow of the hill on which the town was built, in order to throw him down the cliff. But he walked right through the crowd and went on his way.

Then he went down to Capernaum, a town in Galilee, and on the Sabbath began to teach the people. They were amazed at his teaching, because his message had authority.

In the synagogue there was a **man possessed by a demon**, an evil spirit. He cried out at the top of his voice, "Ha! What do you want with us, Jesus of Nazareth? Have you come to destroy us? I know who you are — the Holy One of God!"

"Be quiet!" Jesus **said sternly**. "Come out of him!" Then the demon threw the man down before them all and came out without injuring him.

All the people were amazed and said to each other, "What is this teaching? With authority and power he gives orders to evil spirits and they come out!" And the news about him spread throughout the surrounding area.

Jesus left the synagogue and went to the home of Simon. Now Simon's mother-in-law was suffering from a high fever, and they asked Jesus to help her. So he bent over her and **rebuked** the fever, and it left her. She got up at once and began to wait on them.

When the sun was setting, the people brought to Jesus all who had various kinds of sickness, and laying his hands on each one, he healed them. Moreover, demons came out of many people, shouting, "You are the Son of God!" But he rebuked them and would not allow them to speak, because they knew he was the Christ.

At daybreak Jesus went out to a solitary place. The people were looking for him and when they came to where he was, they tried to keep him from leaving them. But he said, "I must preach the good news of the kingdom of God to the other towns also, because that is why I was sent." And he kept on preaching in the synagogues of Judea.

(Luke 4:14-44)

▼ ▼ ▼ ▼ ▼ ▼ ▼ ▼ ▼ ▼ ▼ ▼ ▼ ▼ ▼ ▼ ▼ ▼ ▼

Understanding the Text   20 minutes

3. a. Why do you think the Holy Spirit descended upon Jesus at
   His baptism? (That is, why at His baptism and not at some
   other time, such as when He was a younger man, or while
   He was praying alone?) And why did the Spirit descend at all?

   b. What was the Father's role in Jesus' baptism?

4. John said that when Christ came to baptize, He would do it
   with the Holy Spirit and *with fire*. Yet when Jesus was
   Himself baptized, the Holy Spirit came *as a dove*. What do
   these two very different images communicate about the
   Spirit?

5. Jesus announced Himself as the one anointed and Spirit-
   filled to proclaim God's good news. Read the note for
   "anointed" on page 42. In what ways was Jesus' baptism
   similar to anointing?

6. a. Luke said Jesus returned to Galilee "in the power of the
   Spirit." What does this mean?

b. Why do you think this was an important fact to mention?

7. From what you can see in Luke 4, how did "the power of the Spirit" affect Jesus' ministry?

8. a. What did Jesus *tell* about His ministry in the synagogue of Nazareth?

b. How did Jesus *show* the same message when He went on to Capernaum?

9. Why didn't Jesus demonstrate the power of the Spirit in Nazareth?

10. The words "power" and "authority" recur several times in Luke 4. What points does this series of events make about . . .

Jesus' power?

Jesus' authority?

Applying the Text   20 minutes

Jesus said, "I tell you the truth, anyone who has faith in me will do what I have been doing. He will do even greater things than these, because I am going to the Father" (John 14:12). He then went on to talk about the Counselor He would send (the passage we studied in session 1). Christians continue to debate what "greater things" Jesus has for us to do.

11. a. In what ways is Jesus' ministry our ministry?

   b. In what ways was His Galilean ministry unique?

12. What do you think it should look like for us to minister "in the power of the Spirit"? In what ways is Luke 4 a model for us?

Assignment

We know that as Christians, we are to be like Jesus (Romans 8:29). We are to have Christlike character and we are to proclaim the message of the good news. But many of us can't believe that we are also to be doing what Jesus had been doing. Copy Luke 4:18-19 ("The Spirit of the Lord is upon me. . . .") onto a card to carry with you. Pray through it at least once a day this week. Ask God to show you how He has anointed and sent you. Ask Him to show you what it will mean for you to minister in the power of the Spirit.

Prayer 5 minutes

While Jesus was praying, the Holy Spirit descended upon Him as a dove and dramatically enabled Him to minister with power and authority. While He was unique in His mission on earth, His followers are called to continue much of what He started, to preach good news to the poor, proclaim freedom for the prisoners, recovery of sight for the blind, and release of the oppressed. Use the promise in John 14:12 or the quotation from Isaiah in Luke 4:18-19, and pray that God would anoint you with the Holy Spirit to do the things that Jesus did, and even greater things.

Reference Notes

Setting: For thirty years Jesus was just Jesus of Nazareth, son of a local carpenter. Then He made the transition from private to public life. He journeyed from His village in the Galilee south to Judea, where His cousin John was baptizing. Then He returned to Galilee, but now He chose as His home base the village of Capernaum, some dozen miles from Nazareth. (In those days when people traveled on foot or didn't travel, twelve miles seemed farther than it does now.) Rumors spread that He was working miracles. On a visit back to His hometown, He was welcomed as a celebrity.

John: Jesus' cousin was the first capital-P Prophet that Israel had seen in four hundred years, and he was creating a huge stir. It was customary to baptize Gentiles when they converted to Judaism since Gentiles needed to be cleansed of sin, but John shocked people by saying that even Jews needed to be cleansed. John prepared the way for Jesus by exposing the people's sins, warning them of judgment, and so revealing their need for a Savior on more than just a political level. The people needed to hear and understand the bad news before they could fully respond to the good news.

Holy Spirit: Luke seems to have had a particular interest in the Holy Spirit since he mentioned the Spirit much more often in his Gospel than did Matthew or Mark. (See, for example, Luke 1:15,35; 2:25-35; 4:1,14,18; 11:13; 24:49).

Jesus was baptized too: Although John's baptism was for repentance, Jesus still sought it out. This wasn't because He needed to repent from sin, but to demonstrate His humble submission to the Father.

dove: In Scripture, the dove often represented innocence or purity (for instance, "innocent as doves," Matthew 10:16). By contrast, fire often represented judgment or purification.

power: The word "power" (Greek: *dynamis*) also occurs more often in Luke than in Matthew and Mark.

synagogue: It was in Jesus' day common for respected visitors to be invited to read from the Scriptures and teach. Jesus did not choose which book to read. The entire book of Isaiah probably could not fit on one scroll, but providentially, Jesus was given the last section of the book. He chose to read the first few verses of chapter 61. By standing up, He indicated He wanted to read, and by sitting down He indicated He was about to teach.

anointed: To anoint someone was to pour oil on him, normally on his head. The Jews did this for prophets, priests, and kings — anyone who was being set apart for a task with special authority from God. Sacred objects, such as items in the temple, were also anointed. The oil symbolized the Spirit of God making the person or object holy (Exodus 30:22-29) and empowered for service (1 Samuel 16:12-13). Ultimately, God was the one who anointed the person (1 Samuel 10:1).
 The prophets had promised that someday Israel would again have a king from the family of David. Because kings were anointed, that promised king was popularly called "the Anointed One" (Hebrew: *mashiach* or Messiah; Greek: *christos* or Christ). Jesus was literally anointed twice by women during His ministry (Luke 7:36-38; John 12:1-7; in both instances, the women chose to anoint His lowly feet rather than His head), but His ministry was inaugurated by baptism.

widow in Zarephath . . . Naaman the Syrian: These two Old Testament stories angered the people of Nazareth because they were accounts of God extending His grace to non-Israelites, whom the Jews despised. The prophets Elijah and Elisha did

42

miracles among the Gentiles because the Israelites were rebellious. The people of Nazareth didn't care for what Jesus' words implied about them.

man possessed by a demon: The Gospels record many demon possessions and demon expulsions. Jesus' presence seemed to bring demons out of the woodwork. The coming of God's kingdom in Jesus' ministry declared war on Satan and his kingdom (Luke 11:20, Colossians 2:15, 1 John 3:8).

The Greek in Luke 4:33 is literally "a man having a demon." While such a phrase is often translated "demon possession," the Greek is less precise. The term "possession" comes from medieval theology and is not found in the Scriptures. It may be more accurate to say that the man in Luke 4 possesses the demon. Thirteen times in the Gospels, the Greek word *daimonizomai* is used. It is also translated as "demon-possession," although the meaning in the Greek is unclear. The New Testament portrays a wide range of demonic influence, from the Gerasene demoniac (Luke 8:26-39), whose behavior was constantly strange and dangerous, to the man in Luke 4, who must have seemed normal most of the time or he presumably would have been barred from the synagogue service.

said sternly . . . rebuked: The Greek verb *epitimao* is used in 4:35,39,41 — twice with regard to demons and once with regard to a fever. It means to sternly reprimand or express disapproval.

---

1. R. A. Torrey, *What the Bible Teaches* (Old Tappan, N.J.: Revell, 1898), p. 94.
2. Joachim Jeremias, *New Testament Theology* (New York: Scribners, 1971), p. 85.

Demonstrations of Power: The Apostles and the Spirit

Acts 3:1–4:4, 9:32-43

This was the generation whose preaching [of Peter and Stephen and Philip and Paul] was more anointed than the preaching of any generation following. If any preaching was the power of God unto salvation and did not need accompanying signs and wonders, it was this preaching. Moreover, this was the generation with more immediate and compelling evidence of the truth of the resurrection than any generation since. Hundreds of eyewitnesses to the risen Lord were alive in Jerusalem. If any generation in the history of the church knew the power of preaching and the authentication of the gospel from first-hand evidence of the resurrection, it was this one. Yet it was they who prayed passionately for God to stretch forth His hand in signs and wonders.[1]

▼ ▼ ▼ ▼ ▼ ▼ ▼ ▼ ▼ ▼ ▼ ▼ ▼ ▼ ▼ ▼ ▼ ▼

Overview   5 minutes

❶ *Ask someone to read the following aloud.*

Dan Shaw was a missionary with Wycliffe Bible Translators in Papua, New Guinea. An elderly man named Hagowanobiayo (hereafter referred to as "H.") had become Dan's close friend and assistant as he worked to translate the Bible into the Samo language. In 1975, H. became seriously ill with malaria. He tried

45

tribal rituals and cultural traditions to heal himself but only grew worse. Dan supplied him with medication, but this didn't help either. Eventually, H. was confined to bed. Dan would bring him portions of Scripture and together they would work on translating.

One afternoon, Dan brought John 5:1-15. After reading him the healing story of the paralytic, H. cried, "That's me! That's me!" He turned to Dan. "I want you to ask Jesus to heal me."

Dan became desperate inside. "I'm just a Baptist boy from Tucson," he thought. "This isn't in my bag of tricks." But in the face of H.'s faith, he felt he had to. He mumbled a short prayer and then went home. He and his wife together sought the Lord. "Your name is on the line," they prayed. "You've got to come through!"

Three days later, to the entire village's amazement, H. was up, walking with a cane. When he informed Dan that Jesus had healed him, Dan skeptically suggested that credit probably belonged to the medication or one of the tribal rituals. Stunned, H. poked him in the ribs with his cane and with great deliberation said, "DON'T YOU BELIEVE?" As a result of H.'s healing, many in the village came to Christ. He lived several more years and was a leader in the village church.[2]

What did Hagowanobiayo understand that missionary Dan Shaw did not? He understood that those who call themselves disciples of Jesus are to do the same things that Jesus did. Jesus' first disciples understood this as well. They knew that to be a disciple meant changing and becoming like the Master. They spent hours with the Master, watching, listening, and absorbing all that He said and did. Eventually, they changed, and when people looked at them, they saw the Master.

Jesus worked to reproduce Himself in His disciples, to make them His extension into the world. "He who listens to you listens to me; he who rejects you rejects me; but he who rejects me rejects him who sent me" (Luke 10:16). "I tell you the truth, whatever you did for one of the least of these brothers of mine, you did for me" (Matthew 25:40). Paul echoed this when he described his team as "Christ's ambassadors" through whom Christ was making His appeal to the world.

(2 Corinthians 5:20)

As we saw in Luke 4, Jesus healed the sick and cast out demons as signs that the kingdom of God had arrived. Sometime later He instructed His followers to do the same works (Luke 9:1-6, 10:1-17). After His resurrection, He sent His disciples to make more disciples and told them to teach the new ones "to obey everything I have commanded you" (Matthew 28:20). This legacy from Master to disciple and from disciple to disciple raises some questions: Does Jesus expect us to obey His commands to heal the sick, drive out demons, and preach the kingdom? What will ministry "in the power of the Spirit" look like for each of us as individuals and for us as gathered bodies of believers?

We began asking these questions in session 3. In this session we will continue to explore them as we look at the ministries of Peter and others in Acts 3 and 9.

Beginning   10 minutes

1. Share the results of your assignment from session 3. What happened when you prayed and thought about ministering in the power of the Spirit? What questions do you have about this subject as you begin this new session?

The Text   5 minutes

At the end of Acts 2, Luke summarized how the movement was doing: The Holy Spirit had been poured out, Peter had preached his first sermon, three thousand were saved in one day, and more were saved with each passing day. Things were going great! In addition, "many wonders and miraculous signs were done by the apostles" (2:43). Acts 3-4 describe one of those signs and its effect on the people and the religious leaders.

Acts 9 jumps several years later. By this time, persecution in Jerusalem had sent disciples fleeing throughout Palestine.

Through them, the Holy Spirit had carried the message of Christ to many Jewish villages. Then persecution waned when one of the leading anti-Jesus agitators, Saul of Tarsus, switched sides and became a follower of Christ. In this period of peace, Peter was free to travel throughout the region, visiting villages where there were disciples.

❶ *Have someone read aloud the two passages below. You may also want to read some or all of the reference notes on pages 55-57.*

One day Peter and John were going up to the temple **at the time of prayer**—at three in the afternoon. Now a man **crippled from birth** was being carried to **the temple gate called Beautiful**, where he was put every day **to beg** from those going into the temple courts. When he saw Peter and John about to enter, he asked them for money. Peter looked straight at him, as did John. Then Peter said, "Look at us!" So the man gave them his attention, expecting to get something from them.

Then Peter said, "Silver or gold I do not have, but what I have I give you. **In the name of Jesus Christ of Nazareth**, walk." Taking him by the right hand, he helped him up, and instantly the man's feet and ankles became strong. He jumped to his feet and began to walk. Then he went with them into the temple courts, walking and jumping, and praising God. When all the people saw him walking and praising God, they recognized him as the same man who used to sit begging at the temple gate called Beautiful, and they were filled with **wonder and amazement** at what had happened to him.

While the beggar held on to Peter and John, all the people were astonished and came running to them in the place called Solomon's Colonnade. When Peter saw this, he said to them: "Men of Israel, why does this surprise you? Why do you stare at us as if by our own power or godliness we had made this man walk? The God of Abraham, Isaac and Jacob, the God of our fathers, has glorified his servant Jesus. You handed him over to be killed, and you disowned him before Pilate, though he had decided to let him go. You disowned the Holy and Righteous One and asked that a murderer be released to you. You killed the author of life, but God raised Him from the dead. We are witnesses of this. By faith in the name of Jesus, this man whom you see and know was made strong. It is Jesus' name and the faith that comes through Him that has given this complete healing to him, as you can all see. . . .

The priests and the captain of the temple guard and the **Sadducees** came up to Peter and John while they were speaking to the people. They were greatly disturbed because the apostles were teaching the people and proclaiming in Jesus the resurrection of the dead. They seized Peter and John, and because it was evening, they put them in jail until the next day. But many who heard the message believed, and the number of men grew to about five thousand (Acts 3:1–4:4).

As Peter traveled about the country, he went to visit the saints in **Lydda.** There he found a man named **Aeneas**, a paralytic who had been bedridden for eight years. "Aeneas," Peter said to him, "**Jesus Christ heals you**. Get up and take care of your mat."

Immediately Aeneas got up. All those who lived in Lydda and Sharon saw him and turned to the Lord.

In **Joppa** there was a disciple named Tabitha (which, when translated, is Dorcas), who was always doing good and helping the poor. About that time she became sick and died, and **her body was washed and placed in an upstairs room**. Lydda was near Joppa; so when the disciples heard that Peter was in Lydda, they sent two men to him and urged him, "Please come at once!"

Peter went with them, and when he arrived he was taken upstairs to the room. All the widows stood around him, crying and showing him the robes and other clothing that Dorcas had made while she was still with them.

Peter sent them all out of the room; then he got down on his knees and prayed. Turning toward the dead woman, he said, "**Tabitha, get up**." She opened her eyes, and seeing Peter she sat up. He took her by the hand and helped her to her feet. Then he called the believers and the widows and presented her to them alive. This became known all over Joppa, and many people believed in the Lord.

Peter stayed in Joppa for some time with a tanner named Simon.

(Acts 9:2-43)

Understanding the Text   20 minutes

Look first at Acts 3:1–4:4.

2. What can you tell from the text about Peter's reasons for healing the disabled man?

3. The healing of the beggar was instantaneous, correcting a life-long disability. Note specifically everything that Peter said and did in the healing.

   a. Which of his words and actions were similar to things Jesus did when He healed people?

   b. What do you observe that was different from Jesus' approach?

4. This miraculous healing was done out in the open with many people around. Describe the scene immediately following the healing.

   a. How did the man respond?

b. How did the crowd respond?

c. How did the religious authorities respond?

d. How would you compare these various responses to what Jesus experienced when He healed people?

5. Jesus' ministry was show-and-tell: demonstration and proclamation. How was Peter's ministry similar?

6. a. The text doesn't mention the Holy Spirit. What do you think was the Spirit's role in this event?

b. What was Jesus' role?

Now look at Acts 9:32-43.

7. What information does the text give us about Aeneas?

8. How was Aeneas healed?

9. What happened in Joppa?

10. Why do you suppose the disciples in Joppa sent for Peter to raise Dorcas from the dead, even though Acts doesn't record him having done this before?

11. a. Note the details of what Peter did in Joppa. Compare them with what Jesus did in Luke 8:49-56. What similarities do you find?

   b. Why do you think the details are so similar?

12. None of the believers in Lydda told Aeneas, "Jesus Christ heals you." Peter did. Likewise, the disciples in Joppa sent for Peter rather than inviting the Holy Spirit to act. The text doesn't say why only Peter healed the sick and raised the dead in these particular instances. Which of the following seem like possible reasons?
   ❐ The Spirit empowered only apostles to raise the dead.
   ❐ The other disciples didn't know the Spirit could do the same things through them.
   ❐ Peter had seen Jesus heal and raise the dead, so he knew *how* to go about these things.
   ❐ Peter had seen Jesus heal and raise the dead, and he *believed* God could do the same things through him.
   ❐ Nobody else in Lydda or Joppa had the gift of healing.
   ❐ God wanted the other disciples to recognize Peter's special status.
   ❐ Other (your ideas):

13. What effect did these "demonstrations of power" have on the people in Lydda and Joppa?

Applying the Text   20 minutes

To demonstrate means "to show clearly or to prove by evidence." There are many ways the Holy Spirit demonstrated the truth of the gospel in the book of Acts. For example, He healed and transformed the lives of people wounded by sin and sickness (Acts 5:12-16). He worked through acts of kindness and service, such as those done by Dorcas. He even brought powerful judgment (Acts 13:9-12) and performed unexplainable miracles (Acts 8:39). Some things He did quickly and other things He did over time.

14. a. What do you think demonstrations of the Spirit's power should look like today?

   b. What are some examples of demonstrations of the Spirit from your own life?

15. In some cases we interpret biblical texts in light of our own personal experiences or training. In what ways do you think your personal experiences affect your interpretation of the "signs and wonders" passages we've just studied?

In the thirteenth century, a monastic scholar named Thomas Aquinas once called upon Pope Innocent II. The Pope was counting a large sum of money and commented to Aquinas, "The church can no longer say, 'Silver and gold have I none.'" "That is true," replied Aquinas, "and neither can she now say, 'Arise and walk.'"

Concerning the healing of the lame man outside the temple, it has been said that "the power was Christ's but the hand was Peter's."[3] Peter worked in cooperation with the Spirit. If he hadn't stopped, addressed the man, and stretched out his hand to him, the Spirit would not have been able to demonstrate His power through healing. There is no doubt, however, that Peter and the other disciples had a tremendous advantage over us today. They had spent three years watching Jesus heal the sick and cast out demons. When presented with a sick person, Peter just naturally imitated what he had seen Jesus do dozens of times before, thus allowing the Spirit to work.

16. a. In what ways should Jesus, Peter, and the other apostles we read about in Scripture be models for us today?

b. Have you ever personally "cooperated" with the Spirit while ministering to someone? Explain.

Assignment

Applying the stories in Acts to our modern situation isn't that simple. Luke's goal in writing was to tell us what happened *then*, not necessarily what should happen *today*. For example, we read in Acts about believers breaking bread (communion), baptizing new converts, and "having everything in common" (see Acts 2:44-45). Today, Christians still take communion and practice baptism, but few have all their belongings in common.

It's important, therefore, to determine which stories may have *precedent* for us today and which may simply be recording the history of the early church.

One way to determine precedent is to see if a particular activity is *commanded* elsewhere in Scripture and if there is a *pattern* of this activity with God's people.

The following passages touch on the issues we've studied in this session. As you read them over during the coming week, decide if you think these kinds of "demonstrations of the Spirit's power" are models for us today, or if they are simply recorded history. Be prepared to discuss your conclusions with the group next week, including how you arrived at your decision. If you view these things as models, what do you think your group should do about it?

▶ Matthew 28:18-20
▶ Luke 9:1-6
▶ Luke 10:1,9
▶ Acts 5:12-16
▶ Acts 6:8

▶ Acts 8:5-7
▶ Acts 14:3
▶ Acts 19:11-12
▶ Hebrews 2:3-4
▶ Galatians 3:5

▼ ▼ ▼ ▼ ▼ ▼ ▼ ▼ ▼ ▼ ▼ ▼ ▼ ▼ ▼ ▼ ▼ ▼ ▼ ▼

Prayer   5 minutes

Spend time as a group honestly confessing anything that may be hindering the Holy Spirit from working powerfully through you. Specifically renounce any teachings or experiences that may be undermining your ability to wholeheartedly believe God's Word. Pray that God would fill you with the faith you need to be His disciples.

▼ ▼ ▼ ▼ ▼ ▼ ▼ ▼ ▼ ▼ ▼ ▼ ▼ ▼ ▼ ▼ ▼ ▼ ▼ ▼

Reference Notes

at the time of prayer: The earliest believers continued to observe the religious duties of Judaism (see Acts 2:46). There were set times every day for sacrifices and prayer in the temple. Questions about Christ's sacrifice replacing these sacrifices had probably not yet arisen.

crippled from birth: Luke provides this information, as well as the man's age in Acts 4:22 (over forty years old), so as to underscore the magnitude of the miracle.

the temple gate called Beautiful: This was probably the main entrance from the Court of the Gentiles on the eastern side of the temple. It was seventy-five feet tall and covered with bronze, hence its name.

to beg: Almsgiving was considered meritorious, so pious Jews on their way to the temple would be the most inclined to give. The disabled man strategically chose his spot for begging.

In the name of Jesus Christ of Nazareth: Peter was not just reciting a formula. He was acting on behalf of Christ, saying and doing what Christ Himself would have done, much as an ambassador acts on behalf of the country he represents. Peter was acting within the limits of the authority Christ had delegated to him (Luke 9:1-2).

wonder and amazement: This was a common response to miracles (Luke 4:36; 5:9,26; 7:16), but it was not the same thing as understanding the miracle's significance, nor the same as saving faith.

Sadducees: One of several Jewish factions active at that time. The Sadducees were small in number, but the richest priestly families were Sadducees, and they controlled the temple with its lucrative trade in sacrifices, as well as the high priesthood. The Pharisees believed that godly Jews would be raised from the dead when the Messiah came in His Kingdom, but the Sadducees rejected the doctrine of resurrection. This was an ongoing and hot debate between the Pharisees and Sadducees, so it's not surprising that the Sadducees were incensed to hear Peter and John teaching about a resurrection.

Lydda . . . Joppa: Joppa was an important port city on the Mediterranean Sea. Lydda was a small town just north of the road between Jerusalem and Joppa.

Aeneas: This man was probably a Christian since Peter's mission was to "visit the saints."

Jesus Christ heals you: The Greek verb tense literally means, "This moment Jesus Christ heals you."

her body was washed and placed in an upstairs room: This was somewhat unusual because there is no mention of anointing the body for burial, which would have been customary. The upstairs room was where the prophets Elijah and Elisha both raised boys from the dead (1 Kings 17:19; 2 Kings 4:10,21). Perhaps the Christians in Joppa were expecting something.

Tabitha, get up: In Aramaic this phrase, *Tabitha cumi,* is only one letter different from the command Jesus issued to Jairus' daughter, *Talitha cumi* (Mark 5:41, KJV).

---

1. John Piper, "Signs and Wonders: Another View," *The Standard* (October 1991), p. 23.
2. This story was taken from Jane Rumph, *Stories from the Front Lines* (Grand Rapids, Mich.: Baker, 1996), pp. 49-52.
3. John R. W. Stott, *The Message of Acts* (Downers Grove, Ill.: InterVarsity, 1990), p. 91.

We Are God's Temple: The Spirit's Holy Presence

1 Corinthians 3:1-17; 6:12-20

Don't grieve God. Don't break his heart. His Holy Spirit, moving and breathing in you, is the most intimate part of your life, making you fit for himself. Don't take such a gift for granted.
—Ephesians 4:30, MSG

▼ ▼ ▼ ▼ ▼ ▼ ▼ ▼ ▼ ▼ ▼ ▼ ▼ ▼
Overview   10 minutes

❶ *Take a few minutes to allow people to share what they heard from the Holy Spirit while reading the Scriptures or in some other situation this week. Then ask someone to read the following aloud.*

I can still remember the first time I felt I was in the presence of God. I was at a large conference of Messianic Jews called "Shekinah '74" that was being held at Columbia University. The speaker that night taught for about an hour on the ark of the covenant. When he finished, there was a time of prayer, and the entire room (about a thousand people) got down on their knees.

Then someone began to share what I took to be a message from God. I will never forget the opening words: "Do you understand what it took for a Holy God to bear His arm and come down to save you?" The entire room broke out in weeping and repentance before the Lord. I felt as if God Himself had come into the room and I dared not raise my head or open my eyes. In my mind were images of the people of Israel, trembling at the foot of Mt. Sinai, telling Moses to go talk to God for them.

Today as I look back on that experience, I realize how appropriate it was that I felt the presence of God at a conference entitled "Shekinah" and after hearing a message on the ark of the covenant. *Shekinah* is a Hebrew word that rabbis have used to signify God's presence, what the Bible calls His "glory." The place that God chose for His Shekinah glory to dwell was in the innermost part of the tabernacle, between the cherubim on the ark of the covenant (1 Samuel 4:4).

This theme of God's presence is woven throughout the Bible. In the beginning God dwells with His creation in the garden. In the end, in the New Jerusalem, God's dwelling will be with men and women and He will live with them (Genesis 3:8, Revelation 21:3). God's presence was the distinctive mark of Israel (Exodus 33:15-16), and His presence regularly filled the tabernacle and the temple (Exodus 40:34-35; 1 Kings 8:11).

It is against this Old Testament backdrop of God's presence that we as New Testament believers are to understand both Christ and the Holy Spirit. Matthew refers to Jesus as Immanuel or "God with us" (Matthew 1:23), and John writes that in Jesus, "the Word became flesh and made his dwelling among us" (John 1:14). Jesus even referred to Himself as the temple (John 2:19), suggesting that He was the presence of God on earth. The Holy Spirit is a continuation of this presence, a presence that Jesus promised would be with us forever (John 14:16).

As we turn our study to the writings of Paul, we will explore some of the implications of having God's presence within and among us, both as individuals and corporately as the body of Christ.

Beginning   10 minutes

1. When, if ever, have you sensed the presence of God?
   - ❏ In certain times of worship
   - ❏ In nature
   - ❏ While reading the Bible
   - ❏ While praying
   - ❏ In certain music
   - ❏ In certain moments with family or friends
   - ❏ When facing up to sin in my life
   - ❏ While hearing a powerful speaker
   - ❏ While going about the routine business of my day
   - ❏ I'm not sure
   - ❏ I don't think I've ever sensed God's presence
   - ❏ Other:

The Text   5 minutes

Paul was frustrated with the believers in Corinth. He wrote them a long letter rebuking them for a series of problems in their community. The two passages here address two different problems. In both cases, the Corinthians' sin showed they fundamentally misunderstood the implications of having the Holy Spirit present among them. In the first case, they didn't understand what it meant to be a community in which the Spirit dwelled. In the second case, they didn't understand what it meant to be individuals in whom the Spirit dwelled.

❶ *Have someone read the following passages aloud. You may also want to read some or all of the reference notes on pages 66-68.*

Brothers, I could not address you as **spiritual** but as **worldly**—mere **infants** in Christ. I gave you milk, not solid food, for you were not yet ready for it. Indeed, you are still not ready. You are still worldly. For since there is jealousy and quarreling among you, are you not worldly? Are you not acting like mere men? For when one says, "I follow Paul," and another, "I follow **Apollos**," are you not mere men?

What, after all, is Apollos? And what is Paul? Only servants, through whom you came to believe — as the Lord has assigned to each his task. I planted the seed, Apollos watered it, but God made it grow. So neither he who plants nor he who waters is anything, but only God, who makes things grow. The man who plants and the man who waters have one purpose, and each will be rewarded according to his own labor. For we are God's fellow workers; **you are God's field, God's building**.

By the grace God has given me, I laid a foundation as an **expert** builder, and someone else is building on it. But each one should be careful **how he builds**. For no one can lay any foundation other than the one already laid, which is Jesus Christ. If any man builds on this foundation using **gold, silver, costly stones, wood, hay or straw**, his work will be shown for what it is, because the Day will bring it to light. It will be revealed with fire, and the fire will test the quality of each man's work. If what he has built survives, he will receive his reward. If it is burned up, he will suffer loss; he himself will be saved, but only as one escaping through the flames.

Don't you know that **you yourselves** are God's temple and that God's Spirit lives in you? If anyone destroys God's temple, God will destroy him; for God's temple is sacred, and you are that temple (1 Corinthians 3:1-17).

"**Everything is permissible for me**"—but not everything is beneficial. "Everything is permissible for me" — but I will not be mastered by anything. **"Food for the stomach and the stomach for food"**—but God will destroy them both. The **body** is not meant for sexual immorality, but for the Lord, and the Lord for the body. By his power God raised the Lord from the dead, and he will raise us also. Do you not know that **your bodies are members of Christ himself**? Shall I then take the members of Christ and **unite** them with a prostitute? Never! **Do you not know** that he who unites himself with a prostitute is one with her in body? For it is said, "The two will become one flesh." But he who unites himself with the Lord is one with him in spirit.

Flee from sexual immorality. **All other sins** a man commits are outside his body, but he who sins sexually sins against his own body. Do you not know that your body is a temple of the Holy Spirit, who is in you, whom you have received from

God? You are not your own; you were bought at a price.
Therefore honor God with your body.

(1 Corinthians 6:12-20)

Understanding the Text   20 minutes

2. What is a temple?

3. Paul tells the Corinthian believers that they are spiritual
   babies. On what does he base this charge?

4. The Corinthian believers as a group are God's temple in
   which the Holy Spirit dwells. Why are jealousy and quarreling in God's temple unacceptable?

5. What does Paul want the Corinthians to understand about
   leaders like Apollos and him? What words does Paul use to
   describe himself and Apollos?

6. List everything Paul says about God in 3:1-17. What is God's
   role in building and maintaining His temple?

7. The presence of the Holy Spirit in the community makes the
   community holy. Likewise, the presence of the Holy Spirit in
   an individual's body makes that body holy. According to
   chapter 6, how were the Corinthians ignoring the sacredness
   of their bodies?

63

8. a. According to Paul, who owns a believer's body?

b. What gives the owner the right to own that body?

c. How does Paul's teaching about the body differ from our society's beliefs about the body?

9. When Paul says that sexual partners "unite" or become "one flesh," he's not talking about something trivial or temporary. What does he mean?

10. a. Why is the misuse of sex a sin against one's own body?

b. Why is sexual sin different from every other kind of sin?

▼ ▼ ▼ ▼ ▼ ▼ ▼ ▼ ▼ ▼ ▼ ▼ ▼ ▼ ▼ ▼ ▼ ▼ ▼

Applying the Text   20 minutes

In previous sessions, you've looked at the Spirit's presence mainly as a source of power to do God's work. In this session, you've focused how the Holy Spirit's presence affects moral choices. Some behavior is inconsistent with the presence of a Being who is as holy as He is powerful.

11. a. What are the implications of the Holy Spirit's presence in a group of Christians?

   b. individual Christians?

12. a. What evidence do you see of the Spirit's presence in your fellowship circle?

   b. in your life personally?

13. The Corinthians seem to have been starkly unaware of the presence of the Holy One in their midst. They thought they were following the Spirit because their meetings were marked by lots of "spiritual" activity, but Paul said they were actually following the flesh because their lives were marked by sin. What do you think leads to that kind of blindness?

14. The Holy Spirit did great signs and wonders in the earliest church, but there was a cost for God's manifest presence. Ananias and Sapphira died because of their willful sin (Acts 5:1-11), and the Corinthians were falling ill and dying because of their sin (1 Corithians 11:30). How would your life be different if the Spirit lived among you with much more power *and* a much higher standard for holiness?

Assignment

In the opening quote for this chapter (Ephesians 4:30), Paul warns the Christians in Ephesus "not to grieve the Holy Spirit of God." Over the coming week, read through Ephesians 4:1-5:21. Make a list of all the behaviors and attitudes Paul is discouraging (things that might grieve the Spirit). Then make a corresponding list of all the attitudes and behaviors he recommends (things that would bring the Spirit joy). From these two lists, which specific behaviors and attitudes do you need to weed out of your life and which ones do you need to begin cultivating?

Prayer   10 minutes

This study may have brought to light ways that group members have been "destroying God's temple." Some sins are less appropriate to confess in a group setting than other sins. It may be wise to divide by gender into smaller groups. Take about ten minutes to confess to and pray for each other. Focus on taking your failings to the cross and receiving God's forgiveness and cleansing. Reaffirm in prayer a commitment to live as the temple of the Holy Spirit, both corporately and individually.

Another option is to allow five minutes for silent reflection and prayer. Let group members write down what they want to confess to God. Encourage them to speak to someone privately if something is weighing on their hearts.

Reference Notes

Setting: Corinth was a commercial center and a mix of various peoples and cultures. It was also a center of learning in which philosophy and public speaking were highly valued. As a result, certain members of the church looked down on Paul because he presented the gospel without the flashy rhetoric of a Greek philosopher. Also, Corinth was famous for sexual immorality, especially in its renowned temple of Aphrodite, where worshipers honored the goddess of love through ritual sex with sacred prostitutes.

spiritual/worldly: The Greek word *sarkinoi* comes from *sarx,* "flesh." The Corinthians were governed by their flesh or sinful nature, as opposed to being *pneumatikoi,* persons governed by the Holy Spirit.

infants: Paul was not talking about how long the Corinthians had been Christians but rather about thier spiritual immaturity.

Apollos: A Jewish Christian from Egypt, educated both in the Jewish Scriptures and in Greek philosophy (Acts 18:24-28). He went to Corinth to build on Paul's work there after Paul left, and his philosophical training and rhetorical skill apparently led some of the Corinthians to prefer him over Paul. But Paul never believed he was in competition with Apollos, whom he called his "fellow worker" (1 Corinthians 3:9). Rather, it was the Corinthians who divided themselves into Paul fans and Apollos fans.

you are God's field, God's building: "You" here is plural. Paul was referring to the community, not to individual Christians. The "church" in Corinth was probably a network of groups who met in homes, groups numbering between perhaps ten and thirty people each. Paul didn't think of them as separate fields, but as one field, one temple.

expert: "Wise" in Greek. Paul contrasted himself with the Corinthians, who thought themselves wise.

how he builds: Paul was primarily concerned with the quality of the workmanship and not the building materials.

gold, silver, costly stones, wood, hay or straw: The issue was not the relative costliness of these different materials, but whether or not they could stand the test of fire. Paul was also alluding to the materials used in the building of the temple in the Old Testament (see 1 Chronicles 22:14-16, 29:2; 2 Chronicles 3:6; Haggai 2:8-9).

Don't you know . . . Do you not know: Paul used this phrase ten times in this letter alone and only one other time in the rest of his writings (Romans 6:16). It was somewhat sarcastic.

you yourselves: Again, "you" is plural. Paul was referring to the church as a whole. In the entire city of Corinth, with all of its pagan temples, this group was the one and only dwelling for the one true and living God.

"Everything is permissible for me": Paul may have been quoting slogans that the Corinthians were repeating to justify their own behavior. It's possible that they got these phrases from Paul himself, but they misunderstood and misapplied them. One of the Corinthians was actually sleeping with his father's wife (1 Corinthians 5:1, presumably not his mother), and the others were tolerating this behavior. Those others may have been carrying on the loose sexual practices for which Corinth was known.

"Food for the stomach and the stomach for food": The Corinthians may have believed that casual sex was as natural as any other bodily function, such as eating.

body: Hebrews saw the body as good and unified with the soul and spirit. Greeks (Corinth was in Greece) viewed the body and the rest of the material world as existing on a "lower plane" than the spirit. Hence, what a person did with his body didn't matter spiritually.

your bodies are members of Christ himself: The Corinthians probably believed that only their spirits were united with Christ.

unite: The Corinthians did not understand the power of sexual relations. They believed it was trivial: sex involved their bodies, so it did not affect their spirits. Paul, on the other hand, said sex was like glue: the Greek word *kollomenos* is a strong word for "joined" or "bonded together." Illicit sex (fornication, sexual immorality) bonds us to the wrong person and therefore severely contaminates our relationship with God.

All other sins: Paul is not suggesting that other sins like gluttony or drunkenness do not involve the body, but that other sins do not affect us at the core of our being in the same way sexual immorality does.

Winning the Battle with Our Flesh: Living by the Spirit

Romans 7:14,21,24-25; 8:1-14

There is a new law at work in the believer. Like every human being since Adam's fall, Paul was caught in the inevitable principle of sin and death. He could not keep from sinning, and he would eventually die. He was not only legally condemned, but morally corrupt in the eyes of his righteous and holy creator-judge. But now in Christ Jesus his sentence of condemnation had been revoked and a higher principle was operating in him to set him free from the stranglehold of sin. Sin had been choking off his life and causing certain death. The power of sin was like the force of gravity pulling him down to destruction unless a greater force intervened to hold him up. That new force, Paul said, is the Holy Spirit.[1]

Moses' law has right but not might; Sin's law has might but not right; the law of the Spirit has both right and might.[2]

Overview   5 minutes

❶ *Ask someone to read the following aloud.*

I remember joking with some of the students in my college fellowship about the need we had to "cast out that spirit of the flesh." How we wished we could just command our sinful tendencies and corrupt habits to leave us in the same way Jesus commanded

69

the demons to leave their victims. We joked because we knew such a thing was just wishful thinking. Our "flesh," our sinful nature, was something we had to live with yet learn to subdue. As followers of Christ, we needed to gain the upper hand over our flesh, like a wrestler gaining the advantage over his opponent. We need to get on top of our flesh and pin it to the mat!

We can talk about the Spirit's power and presence, but the struggle with the flesh often dominates our lives. When flesh defeats us, we may be tempted to resign ourselves to being spiritual failures. Others seem to be able to live righteous, holy lives, free from sin's domination, but we can't. We just don't have enough discipline and determination.

In the years since my college days, I've observed two problems among Christians when it comes to this subject of the flesh. One is our reluctance to admit that we have any struggles with our flesh at all. Even though the Bible addresses it and everyone experiences it, no one really wants to talk about it. Better to put on a good face and pretend to be living the victorious Christian life. The second problem is our failure to make use of all that God has given us through His Spirit. Perhaps we just don't understand that the promises about the Spirit are real and not too good to be true. Or perhaps we are too individualistic. We find it hard to apprehend and experience the help the Bible says is there for us because we find it hard to be dependent. But in God's economy, it's those who are humble, and who ask, who end up receiving.

As we look this time at Paul's letter to the Romans, we will see a man ecstatic about all that God has done for him in Christ and through His Spirit. We will try to catch his enthusiasm for, and dependence upon, the Spirit in the battle against the flesh.

▼ ▼ ▼ ▼ ▼ ▼ ▼ ▼ ▼ ▼ ▼ ▼ ▼ ▼ ▼ ▼ ▼ ▼ ▼
Beginning   15 minutes

1. Each of us has areas of our lives that frustrate us, that we can't seem to get under control. What are some of the things you've done to try to change your frustrating tendencies?

The Text

In Romans 7-8, Paul describes the struggle between flesh and Spirit. It's a tightly woven passage that goes to the core of where most of us live.

❶ *Have someone read the text aloud. You may also want to read some or all of the reference notes on pages 76-78.*

We know that the law is spiritual; but I am unspiritual, sold as a slave to sin. . . . So I find this law at work: When I want to do good, evil is right there with me. . . . What a wretched man I am! Who will rescue me from this body of death? Thanks be to God—through Jesus Christ our Lord! . . .

Therefore, there is now no **condemnation** for those who are in Christ Jesus, because through Christ Jesus the law of the Spirit of life set me free from the law of sin and death. For what the law was powerless to do in that it was weakened by the **sinful nature**, God did by sending his own Son in **the likeness of sinful man** to be a sin offering. And so he condemned sin in sinful man, in order that the righteous requirements of the law might be **fully met in us**, who do not live according to the sinful nature but **according to the Spirit**.

Those who live according to the sinful nature have their minds set on what that nature desires; but those who live in accordance with the Spirit have their minds set on what the Spirit desires. The mind of sinful man is death, but the mind **controlled by** the Spirit is life and peace; the sinful mind is hostile to God. It does not submit to God's law, nor can it do so. Those controlled by the sinful nature cannot please God.

You, however, are controlled not by the sinful nature but by the Spirit, **if** the Spirit of God lives in you. And if anyone does not have the **Spirit of Christ**, he does not belong to Christ. But if Christ is in you, your **body is dead** because of sin, yet your spirit is alive because of righteousness. And if the Spirit of him who raised Jesus from the dead is living in you, he who raised Christ from the dead will also give life to your mortal bodies through his Spirit, who lives in you.

Therefore, brothers, we have an **obligation**—but it is not to the sinful nature, to live according to it. For if you live according to the sinful nature, you will die; but if by the Spirit you **put**

71

to death the misdeeds of the body, you will live, because those who are led by the Spirit of God are sons of God.

(Romans 7:14,21,24-25; 8:1-14)

▼ ▼

Understanding the Text   20 minutes

2. According to the first paragraph above, what is it about being a follower of Christ that has Paul so frustrated?

3. a. Paul's tone takes a radical shift in chapter 8, from defeat and discouragement to excitement and victory. The shift begins with freedom from condemnation. What does "no condemnation" mean?

   b. Why is that such good news?

Paul uses the word "law" in several ways throughout this passage. First, he uses it to refer to God's commandments as laid out in the Old Testament. This is what Jesus repeatedly referred to as "The Law."

The second law mentioned by Paul is *the law of sin and death*. This law refers to the inevitable consequence of disobeying God's commandments and can be compared to the law of gravity. As surely as you will hit the ground if you jump off a building, so you will die if you sin. What's more, according to this law you *will* sin because the commandments are not strong enough to keep you from doing so.

The third law described by Paul, *the law of the Spirit of life*, is what gives us the power to overcome *the law of sin and death*. It is to this law that Paul turns his attention in this passage.

4. A simple version of the law of gravity is, "If you jump off a building, you will hit the ground." A simple version of the law of sin and death is, "If you sin, you will die—and you will sin." How would you state a simple version of the law of the Spirit of life?

5. a. How have you experienced the law of sin and death?

   b. the law of the Spirit of life?

6. We access the law of the Spirit of life by living "according to the Spirit" rather than "according to the sinful nature." List everything Paul says about what it means to live according to the Spirit.

Living according to the Spirit involves a partnership between the Spirit and us. We don't lie back and passively let the Spirit do all the work. Nor do we "access" the Spirit's power in the same way we "access" electricity by inserting a plug into a wall outlet. We are persons and the Spirit is a person. We work together.

7. a. According to Paul, what does the Spirit do in this partnership?

   b. What do we do?

8. One important element of our partnership with the Spirit is our mindset. We can have a mindset that is "of the flesh" or "of the Spirit."

   a. How would you explain what a mindset is?

   b. What are some of the qualities of a mindset that is led by or focused on the Spirit?

9. What do you think is involved in putting to death the misdeeds of the body? What does this look like on a day-to-day basis?

10. Why do we have to put to death the misdeeds of the body "by the Spirit"? What happens if we try to do this without the Spirit?

▼ ▼ ▼ ▼ ▼ ▼ ▼ ▼ ▼ ▼ ▼ ▼ ▼ ▼ ▼ ▼ ▼ ▼ ▼

Applying the Text   20 minutes

11. What specific things do you notice in your life that tell you whether you are living "according to the Spirit" or "according to the flesh"?

In Romans 8, Paul presents the solution to his cry in 7:24–"Who will deliver me? . . . ." He begins with "no condemnation," ends with "no separation" and in between declares there is "no defeat." [3] It is worth nothing that there is not one single command in chapter 8. Paul simply declares what is true about us as believers–what our position is in Christ. We may "feel" like we are locked in a prison cell because of a particular sin problem, but the truth is, the prison door is wide open. Because of the "the law of the Spirit of life," we are free!

12a. Why do you think it is important for us to first understand this truth before we can win any battles with our flesh?

b. In what ways can believing this truth help you in an area you're struggling?

13. After studying Romans 7 and 8, we can see that God isn't asking us to fix ourselves through sheer willpower and determination. He has sent His Spirit to live inside us and give us the power to change. Consider now some of those areas of frustration you shared at the beginning of this session. How can you begin to work in cooperation with the Spirit to conquer these behaviors or attitudes that you have been unable to bring under control?

▼ ▼ ▼ ▼ ▼ ▼ ▼ ▼ ▼ ▼ ▼ ▼ ▼ ▼ ▼ ▼ ▼ ▼

Assignment

Pick an area of your life where you have battled your flesh yet seen no victory. (For ideas of what Paul means by deeds of the flesh, see Galatians 5:19-21, a passage we will study in session 8.) Identify when or under what circumstances you find yourself most tempted. Decide ahead of time that at those moments you will stop and say a prayer of surrender to and dependence upon the Holy Spirit. Also, decide ahead of time what you need to do practically to "put to death" that particular misdeed. Keep a journal of what happens. If you get frustrated, phone someone in the group.

Prayer   10 minutes

It is clear from this passage in Romans that the key to winning
the battle with our flesh is moment-by-moment dependence
upon and submission to the Spirit of God who dwells in us. Get
into groups of two or three to share specific areas of your life in
which you need help. It may be a good idea to separate the
groups by gender. Then pray that the Spirit of God would give
you life and assist you in putting to death these "misdeeds."

Reference Notes

Setting: Paul's letter to the believers in Rome is his systematic
presentation of the gospel. After explaining why the entire
human race deserves God's wrath, Paul carefully explains how,
through Christ, God has provided an alternative to wrath: grace.
Much of his terminology, such as "righteousness" and "justification," comes from the Jewish and Roman legal worlds. Paul
shows how by faith in Christ, people are declared not guilty
(justified) and then enabled to become like Christ (sanctified).
In Romans chapters 7-8, Paul is focusing on the latter, the
process by which a person becomes free from not just the
penalty for sin, but the habit of sinning.

condemnation: In a legal sense, this includes both the sentence
(guilty of sin) and its consequences (bondage to sin).

sinful nature: The NIV uses this phrase to render the Greek word
sarx, which literally means "flesh." This word was normally used
for man's lower nature—desires for food, sex, money, power,
status, comfort, and so on. These desires don't have to be evil,
but Paul seems to have had in mind natural desires run amok:
swollen and out of control because of people's rebellion against
God.

the likeness of sinful man: Christ was like us in that He was a
real human being with real flesh (that is, a real body and human

desires). However, He differed from us in that He was sinless.
(Hebrews 4:15)

fully met in us: Christ alone perfectly met the requirements of God's Law. Paul is talking here about more than justification (in which Christ's perfect obedience is credited to us). He is also talking about sanctification (in which we actually become able to live out the righteous requirements of the Law). Note that Paul is not saying that *we* meet the requirements. Rather, they are met in us by the Holy Spirit. We can't expect this to occur flawlessly overnight, but we can expect consistent progress year by year.

according to the Spirit: In accordance with or in conformity with the Holy Spirit.

Those: Literally, "those according to the Spirit"—that is, those who at core have their identities defined by their allegiance to the Spirit. Such people have their minds set on what the Spirit desires. It's the nature or identity that determines the mindset, not vice versa.

controlled by: Literally, "*in* the flesh" or "*in* the Spirit" (NASB). The Greek text has no words that imply control or coercion. The Holy Spirit doesn't possess humans and control their minds and actions. To be "in the Spirit" is to be guided, led, directed, even strongly nudged, but not coerced. We always retain the power to go our own way, so we always have the responsibility to choose to obey the Spirit's prompting. By contrast, years of living "in the flesh" creates habits so ingrained that they virtually control us. This is why we do what we don't want to do. We need the powerful intervention of the Holy Spirit to break the control of the flesh so that we can choose to be "in the Spirit." But the longer we live under the Spirit's direction, the more natural that state becomes for us.

if: Paul's "if" here is not calling the Roman believers' salvation into question. He is saying, "If, which is indeed the case."

Spirit of Christ: Paul is not confused when he speaks of "Christ," "the Spirit of Christ," and "the Spirit of God." He sensed both the oneness and the threeness of God, which students of Scripture several centuries later articulated as the Trinity.

body is dead: The meaning of this phrase is disputed. In the context, it seems to refer to our mortal bodies, which are subject to death because of sin.

obligation: This word was normally used for a monetary debt. We don't owe our flesh anything.

put to death: Paul is not suggesting masochism (self-afflicted pain) or asceticism (contempt for natural bodily functions that results in severe self-denial). He refers to an ongoing, continuous activity of "squeezing the life out of" the misdeeds of our flesh. We choke off whatever nourishes them.

---

1. John Rea, *The Holy Spirit in the Bible* (Lake Mary, Fla.: Creation House, 1990), p. 213.
2. Leon Morris, *The Epistle to the Romans* (Grand Rapids, Mich.: Eerdmans, 1988), p. 301.
3. Morris, p. 299.

We Are God's Children: The Witness of the Spirit

Romans 8:12-17

The Spirit itself beareth witness with our spirit, that we are the children of God. This is, beyond any question, one of the most glorious statements concerning Christian experience found anywhere in the Bible from beginning to end. Nothing is more important from the standpoint of experience, from the standpoint of happiness and joy in the Christian life, from the standpoint of enjoying our great salvation. If it can be said that any one verse constitutes the hallmark of the evangelical Christian I would say that it is this one.[1]

▼ ▼ ▼ ▼ ▼ ▼ ▼ ▼ ▼ ▼ ▼ ▼ ▼ ▼ ▼ ▼ ▼ ▼

Overview   10 minutes

❶ *Allow two or three people to share any victories they had over their flesh this week. If sharing the specific sin seems inappropriate (depending on your group's level of frankness), it may be enough for the person to talk about how he or she interacted with the Spirit in the process. Then have someone read the following aloud.*

There is a big difference between the way my two teenagers, Daniel and Sharon, behave in our home and the way their friends do. Often, when they come home from school in the late afternoon, the first thing they do is drop their book bags, jackets, and anything else they are carrying onto the floor just inside the front door. Then they head directly to the refrigerator, which they thoroughly and meticulously explore. Seizing upon several food and drink items, their next and final stop is the family room sofa, upon which they drape themselves in front of the television—without speaking—until dinner.

Their friends, on the other hand, would never do such things in our home. They would only enter the front door when invited in. They would carefully place their things somewhere against the wall, out of the way. They may come into the kitchen but wouldn't dream of opening a cupboard or checking out the refrigerator. The only way they would get anything to eat or drink would be if it was offered to them. And they would probably sit at the kitchen table and engage me in some sort of polite conversation rather than run off to channel surf in our family room.

One explanation for these differences in behavior is that Daniel and Sharon were never taught good manners! Another explanation, though, is that this is their home. They belong there. They are the children. And because they are the children, they know they are always welcome. They know that anything in the kitchen is theirs to have. They know they are free to sit anywhere and do just about anything they want. Their friends, however, won't take these same liberties because their status is different. They don't "belong" in our home. They are not the children. They are the guests.

Daniel and Sharon are pretty secure about their identity as the children in our home. I don't need to remind them constantly because they just seem to know it. They have also come to count on me, as well as my husband, for certain things. They know, for example, that we will always love them, that we will always provide for their needs (but maybe not their wants), that we will care for them when they are sick, that we will comfort them when they are hurt, that we truly want what's best for them, and that we will never abandon them.

According to Paul, as Christians we are called God's children, not His "guests." And we are to *know* we are His children in the same way that Daniel and Sharon know they are my children. As God's children, we enjoy certain privileges and blessings. In this session we will continue in our study of Romans 8 to discover what it means to be children of God and the role the Holy Spirit plays in this relationship. We will also address barriers we may have to living as God's children.

Beginning

10 minutes

1. When you were growing up, how secure were you in your identity as a child who belonged?

2. a. What things in your experience contributed to your feelings of belonging?

   b. What things diminished your feelings of belonging and being accepted?

The Text

5 minutes

In this passage, the topic begins to change from "doing" to "being." Paul shifts his focus away from the sanctifying work of the Holy Spirit in our lives as Christians (how we "do" righteousness) to our identity as Christians (who we are).

❶ *Ask someone to read the text aloud. You may also want to refer to the reference notes on pages 86-87.*

Therefore, brothers, we have an obligation—but it is not to the sinful nature, to live according to it. For if you live according to the sinful nature, you will die; but if by the Spirit you put to

81

death the misdeeds of the body, you will live, because those who are **led** by the Spirit of God are **sons** of God. For you did not receive a spirit that makes you a slave again to fear, but you received the **Spirit of sonship.** And by him we cry, "**Abba, Father.**" The Spirit himself **testifies** with our spirit that we are God's children. Now if we are children, then we are **heirs**—heirs of God and co-heirs with Christ, **if** indeed we share in his sufferings in order that we may also share in his glory.

(Romans 8:12-17)

▼ ▼ ▼ ▼ ▼ ▼ ▼ ▼ ▼ ▼ ▼ ▼ ▼ ▼ ▼ ▼ ▼ ▼ ▼
Understanding the Text   20 minutes

3. In Romans 8:9-11, Paul stated that *having* the Holy Spirit was evidence that we "belong to Christ." Now he says that being *led by* the Spirit is evidence of being "sons of God." What does it mean to be "led by the Spirit"?

4. What does it mean to be a "son" or "child" of God? What information about this identity does the text give?

5. Why do you think it is important for us to have a somewhat objective piece of evidence to assure us of our relationship with God?

6. Paul uses the images of slaves and children (specifically adopted children) to illustrate our experience with the Holy Spirit. How would you describe the differences between slaves and children?

7. a. What might slaves have to fear?

   b. Why do sons or daughters have no reason to fear?

8. God's wrath against evildoers is a good reason to fear God. Why can God's adopted children stop being afraid of God?

9. a. It is the Spirit who enables us to cry "*Abba,* Father." What does it mean to cry out to God as Abba?

   b. What does the Spirit have to do with this? Why can't we cry to God as Abba on our own?

10. According to this passage, how can a person know whether or not he or she is really God's adopted child?

11. How does the Spirit testify with our spirit? What is that like in your experience?

12. a. Children share in the blessings as well as the difficulties of the family to which they belong. The same is true for us as God's children. What are some of the things we get to "share" in the last sentence of this passage?

   b. Why is suffering as a Christian not just a meaningless, painful experience to be avoided at all cost?

Applying the Text

20 minutes

13. Many people feel insecure about their relationship with God. They fear rejection because of their failures, so they maintain a safe distance from God. If Paul were to devote a paragraph in one of his epistles to such people, what do you think he would say?

14. Paul says we can be sure we are God's children if the Spirit is leading us down paths of righteousness. What specific evidence is there in your own life that the Spirit is leading you?

15. When my children were small, they would immediately cry out "mommy" or "daddy" whenever they were afraid or in need. Their response was entirely automatic. According to Paul, we are to automatically cry out "Daddy" to God because of the Spirit's work in our lives. What is your automatic reaction to troubles, fears, and problems? Is it easy for you to cry "Daddy" to God, or do you instinctively avoid contact with Him at such times?

16. Do you feel like a son or daughter of God, or do you feel more like something else (such as a slave or guest)? Why do you think you feel the way you do? What specific things in your life have helped or hindered your sense of being a child of God?

Assignment   5 minutes

There are many ways in which parents can communicate love to their children and make them feel secure. There are objective ways, such as providing for their children's needs (food, shelter, clothing, education). There are also more subjective ways, such as showing comfort, being affectionate, and verbalizing love. God communicates His love to us and causes us to truly know we are His children in many ways as well. Write down the specific ways in which God has personally assured you of your identity as His child. Make note of which "evidences" speak to your intellect and which speak to your heart. Spend time each day this week meditating on these evidences and allow the Holy Spirit to further testify to you that you are a child of God.

Prayer   10 minutes

Childhood experiences can sometimes affect our capacity to experience God as Father in the present, especially in the way Paul has described. If your father was emotionally distant, overly punitive in his discipline, verbally and physically abusive, or never around, you may view God in the same light. Break down into groups of two or three. Share in the smaller group any specific experiences from your own childhood that you feel may be blocking your experience of God today. Invite the Holy Spirit into that memory, allowing Him to bring healing and comfort. Renounce any bitterness towards anyone who has mistreated you. Then pray that the Holy Spirit would, as Paul said, testify with your spirit of your identity as a child of God. (This process will obviously take more than ten minutes to take effect, but beginning it with a group of close, trusted friends can be an important first step.)

Reference Notes

led: Paul is not talking here about guidance as to whom to marry or whether to change jobs. He is talking about being led into right moral choices versus wrong ones. This verse is connected with the previous one about right behavior versus misdeeds. Paul envisions the kind of leading mentioned in Psalm 23:3 ("He leads me in paths of righteousness for his name's sake," KJV).

sons . . . "Sonship" was the normal way to speak of adoption. Jews did not adopt children, so Paul's notions of adoption came from Roman law. A well-to-do Roman man without a male heir could adopt a young man to perpetuate the family name and inherit the estate. Women could not inherit property so no one adopted girls. When Paul wanted to emphasize the legal nature of our adoption, he spoke of us as "sons." Under Roman law, an adopted son had the full rights of a natural son. Toward the end of this paragraph Paul shifted to the more general word, "children," since he was talking about both men and women. It was startling for Christian women to hear Paul saying that with God they had the full legal rights of sons since they did not enjoy those rights in their earthly families.

The true evidence of "sonship," according to Paul, is a life led by the Spirit into righteousness. The language here is emphatic. These people *alone* are the true children of God. Paul is not talking about the universal fatherhood of God. All people are God's offspring via creation, but only those who have been reconciled to Him through the new birth are His true sons and daughters (see John 1:12-13).

Spirit of sonship: The meaning of the word "spirit" in verse Romans 8:15 has been debated. In the context, Paul has been talking about the Holy Spirit. A plausible interpretation could be, "You did not receive the Holy Spirit as a Spirit of bondage but as a Spirit of adoption."[2]

Abba, Father: The intimate Aramaic word for "Papa," and the standard Greek word for "Father." Aramaic and Greek were both spoken in Galilee, where Jesus grew up, and He used this double expression in Mark 14:36 while praying. "Abba" was the familiar way in which Jewish children referred to their fathers at home.

Jesus may have originally taught His disciples to pray in Aramaic, so He may have used this word, Abba, in the Lord's prayer. Jews would not have dared to address God in this manner, but Jesus always did (except in His cry on the cross).

testifies: According to Jewish law, two witnesses were needed to confirm a matter. Paul says that the Spirit Himself, along with our spirits, confirm our status as God's children. This is a subjective, private experience in the heart of the individual believer. (See Galatians 4:6; 1 John 5:6-12.)

heirs: This is not an inheritance in the normal sense. God is not dying and leaving us His estate. Our inheritance is like that of the Levites, who were not given any land or material wealth, but their inheritance was God Himself (see Deuteronomy 18:2). The reason we can be certain of our future inheritance is that the Holy Spirit, whom we have right now, is the down payment (see Romans 8:23).

if: Paul is not suggesting that suffering is optional. Suffering is a certainty for the child of God, in the same way that future glory is a certainty. Suffering and glory are closely linked in the Scripture (see Luke 24:26, 2 Corinthians 4:17, Hebrews 2:9, 1 Peter 5:10).

---

1. D. Martyn Lloyd-Jones, *Romans: The Sons of God, An Exposition of Chapter 8:5-17* (Grand Rapids, Mich.: Zondervan, 1975), p. 285.

2. John Murray, quoted in Leon Morris, *The Epistle to the Romans* (Grand Rapids, Mich.: Eerdmans, 1988), p. 314.

Called to Be Free: The Fruit of the Spirit

Galatians 5:1-26

When the Spirit enters us at the moment of conversion, it is like the Allied invasion of Normandy in World War II. God has returned to occupy what is rightfully His. The more the new believer, like the local French inhabitants of Normandy, cooperates with the "Invader," the sooner the territory once held by the enemy [our flesh] may be reclaimed and fully liberated.[1]

Where love is the compelling power, there is no sense of strain or conflict or bondage in doing what is right: the man or woman who is compelled by Jesus' love and empowered by His Spirit does the will of God from the heart. For (as Paul could say from experience) "where the Spirit of the Lord is, there the heart is free."[2]

▼ ▼ ▼ ▼ ▼ ▼ ▼ ▼ ▼ ▼ ▼ ▼ ▼ ▼ ▼ ▼

Overview   10 minutes

❶ *Take about five minutes to allow a few people to share something they learned or gained from the assignment—noticing ways in which God has communicated to them that they are His children. Then have someone read the following aloud.*

One of my favorite books is *The Screwtape Letters*, by C. S. Lewis. This actual work is a collection of letters from an

89

experienced devil named Screwtape to his young nephew, Wormwood. In these letters, Screwtape tells Wormwood all the tricks of the trade for keeping his "patient" out of "Enemy" hands.

Wormwood's patient unfortunately falls into Enemy hands and becomes a Christian. After Wormwood fails to lure him back to "the Father below," Screwtape writes this:

> My Dear Wormwood,
>
> Through this girl and her disgusting family the patient is now getting to know more Christians every day, and very intelligent Christians too. For a long time it will be quite impossible to remove spirituality from his life. Very well then; we must corrupt it. No doubt you have often practiced transforming yourself into an angel of light as a parade-ground exercise. Now is the time to do it in the face of the Enemy. The World and the Flesh have failed us; a third Power remains. And success of this third kind is the most glorious of all. A spoiled saint, a Pharisee, an inquisitor, or a magician, makes better sport in Hell than a mere common tyrant or debauchee.[3]

What Lewis has expressed so well through the devil, Screwtape, is something many of us need to hear. Spirituality can be easily corrupted. Christianity has a tendency to go bad. What starts as "good news" (the free gift of salvation through faith in Christ) sometimes ends as "bad news" (a long "to do" list of rules and requirements). Paul asked, "After beginning with the Spirit, are you now trying to attain your goal by human effort?" (Galatians 3:3).

We often make this shift as we try to bring our flesh under control. I know this from experience. On more than one occasion, I have set out on a self-improvement campaign that failed. Being a legalist at heart, I employed the "do not handle, do not taste, do not touch" method that Paul says has "the appearance of wisdom" but in reality has "no value in restraining the flesh" (Colossians 2:20-23). Instead of becoming more like Christ, I wound up a prisoner to rules.

The alarming news, however, is not simply that rules don't work. Lewis is on to something. Behind Christian legalism is the activity of evil spirits. Paul told the Galatian believers, who were succumbing to legalistic teaching, that they were actually "bewitched" (Galatians 3:1). Elsewhere, he attributed legalism to the philosophies of "elemental spirits" (Colossians 2:8)[4] or "things taught by demons" (1 Timothy 4:1). Whenever we bring ourselves under false teachings, we forfeit our freedom.

The key to maintaining our freedom while at the same time curbing our flesh is life in the Spirit. It's the Holy Spirit who leads us into all truth (John 14:17), and it is life in the Spirit that sets us free from the bondage to rules and regulations. We look now at Paul's letter to the Galatians to discover the Holy Spirit's role in our liberty.

Beginning

10 minutes

1. When you were a child, were you the kind who usually tried to obey the rules, or did you usually try to find a way around the rules? Share an example with the group.

The Text

❶ *Because this session covers all of Galatians 5, you will read the text in sections, pausing to answer questions.*

It is for **freedom** that Christ has set us free. Stand firm, then, and do not let yourselves be burdened again by a yoke of slavery.

Mark my words! I, Paul, tell you that if you let yourselves be **circumcised**, Christ will be of no value to you at all. Again I declare to every man who lets himself be circumcised that he is obligated to obey the whole **law**. You who are trying to be **justified** by law have been alienated from Christ; you have fallen away from grace. But by faith we eagerly await through the Spirit the righteousness for which we hope. For in Christ Jesus neither circumcision nor uncircumcision has any value. The only thing that counts is faith expressing itself through love.

You were running a good race. Who cut in on you and kept

you from obeying the truth? That kind of persuasion does not come from the one who calls you. "A little yeast works through the whole batch of dough." I am confident in the Lord that you will take no other view. The one who is throwing you into confusion will pay the penalty, whoever he may be. Brothers, **if I am still preaching circumcision**, why am I still being persecuted? In that case the offense of the cross has been abolished. As for those agitators, I wish they would go the whole way and **emasculate themselves**!

You, my brothers, were called to be free. But do not use your freedom to indulge the sinful nature; rather, serve one another in love. The entire law is summed up in a single command: "Love your neighbor as yourself." If you keep on biting and devouring each other, watch out or you will be destroyed by each other.

So I say, live by the Spirit, and you will not gratify the desires of the sinful nature. For the sinful nature desires what is contrary to the Spirit, and the Spirit what is contrary to the sinful nature. They are in conflict with each other, so that you do not do what you want. But if you are led by the Spirit, you are not under law.

The **acts of the sinful nature** are obvious: **sexual immorality, impurity and debauchery; idolatry** and **witchcraft**; hatred, discord, jealousy, fits of rage, selfish ambition, dissensions, factions and envy; drunkenness, orgies, **and the like**. I warn you, as I did before, that those who live like this will not inherit the kingdom of God.

But the **fruit** of the Spirit is love, joy, peace, patience, kindness, goodness, faithfulness, gentleness and self-control. Against such things there is no law. Those who belong to Christ Jesus have crucified the sinful nature with its passions and desires. Since we live by the Spirit, let us keep in step with the Spirit. Let us not become conceited, provoking and envying each other.

(Galatians 5:1-26)

▼ ▼

Understanding the Text   25 minutes

❶ *Have someone read aloud the first two paragraphs of the text above. You may also want to refer to the reference notes on pages 97-98.*

2. Read the note on "freedom" on page 97. What are the Galatians free from?

3. Why will Christ be of no value to the Galatians if they take on the burden of the Jewish ritual system?

4. a. What is the difference between being "justified" by a system of rules and "justified" by grace?

   b. Why are these two ways of approaching God mutually exclusive?

❶ *Have someone read the next two paragraphs of the text.*

5. Explain in your own words the false teaching that the Galatians have received.

6. a. What do you think "the offense of the cross" is?

   b. Why would it abolish "the offense of the cross" if Paul accepted the claim that Gentiles had to become Jews in order to please God?

7. Freedom can be abused. How might the Galatians abuse their freedom?

8. Paul does expect the Galatians to do something. What are they set free for?

9. How is "faith expressing itself through love" different from meeting specific legal criteria (circumcision for the Galatians, perhaps something different for us) in order to be acceptable to God?

❶ *Have someone read the last three paragraphs of the text.*

10. Paul never tells us exactly how living by the Spirit is supposed to look in our lives. Instead he uses phrases like "being led by the Spirit" and "keeping in step with the Spirit." What do these images (*being led by, keeping in step with*) tell us about how to live life in the Spirit?

11. a. Paul tells us that, if we belong to Christ, our flesh or sinful nature has been crucified. What do you think this means?

   b. How does knowing this help us in our battle with sinful desires?

12. Why do you think Paul describes the evidence of the Spirit's work in our lives as *fruit*?

▼ ▼ ▼ ▼ ▼ ▼ ▼ ▼ ▼ ▼ ▼ ▼ ▼ ▼ ▼ ▼ ▼ ▼

Applying the Text   20 minutes

13. Many Christians find it easier to organize their lives around a system of rules and guidelines than to experience the freedom of life in the Spirit. Do you ever see this tendency in your own life? If so, describe how this looks.

14. a. Paul often compared the Christian life to running a race. Here he suggests that someone or something has "cut in" on the Galatians and diverted them away from the race. Why do you think people are so easily diverted away from living by the Spirit?

   b. Do you find yourself easily diverted? If so, what are some of the things that divert you?

15. In what ways have you seen evidence of the Spirit's work in your life, replacing the *acts* of your sinful nature with the *fruit* of His presence?

Assignment

One unifying theme throughout Galatians 5 is love. Paul tells us that our faith should "express itself through love" (verse 6) and that we should not indulge our flesh, but rather "serve one another in love" (verse 13). In fact, like Jesus (Matthew 7:12), Paul sums up the entire law in a single command: "Love your neighbor as yourself." For one week, commit yourself to use love as your guiding principle at home, at work, at school, and within your church family. Seek the Holy Spirit's power to live a life of love. Take some time at the end of each day to review the day prayerfully through the lens of love. Afterward note any changes this commitment made in your relationships with others or within yourself.

Prayer   10 minutes

Choose one of the nine characteristics from the fruit of the Spirit that you feel needs to be more evident in your life. Briefly explain why. Then pray for each other individually. Ask the Holy Spirit specifically to increase this characteristic in each of you and to give you the grace to "keep in step" with Him while He does.

▼ ▼ ▼ ▼ ▼ ▼ ▼ ▼ ▼ ▼ ▼ ▼ ▼ ▼ ▼ ▼ ▼ ▼ ▼

Reference Notes

freedom: Freedom is a major theme in the book of Galatians. Before Paul arrived in Galatia, the readers of this letter were literally enslaved by fear to their pagan religions. If they failed to perform the proper rituals and sacrifices, there would be retribution from their gods (4:8). When they trusted Christ, through the preaching of Paul, they were set free to serve God in the power of His Spirit.

Before long, false teachers infiltrated the church at Galatia, corrupting the simple message of the gospel. The Galatians were enslaved again, but this time it was to the law. They were falsely taught that, in order to follow Christ, they needed to become Jewish and submit to Old Testament rules and regulations. Faith in Christ was not enough.

Paul wrote this letter to straighten them out. They needed to understand all that they were set free *from* (pagan gods and Old Testament rituals) and all that they were set free *for* (bearing the fruit of the Spirit).

circumcised: Circumcision was the rite done on Jewish male infants to demonstrate their membership in the community of Israel. It was also the rite done on any nonJewish male wishing to convert to Judaism. Paul didn't oppose circumcision itself, but what it represented for the Galatians. They were adding circumcision as a necessary requirement for earning salvation. Paul adamantly opposed this. According to him, faith in Christ plus nothing earns salvation.

law: The Jewish ritual system.

justified: Declared righteous and approved by God.

if I am still preaching circumcision: Paul is not suggesting that he ever recommended circumcision as being necessary for salvation. He is saying hypothetically that *if* he had preached this message, he would not be persecuted as he is.

emasculate themselves: Paul waxed sarcastic in his passion for the purity of the gospel. The Jews detested the pagan practice of castrating certain men in religious rituals, yet they demanded that the Galatians be circumcised.

acts of the sinful nature: "Lusts of the flesh" in KJV. Some people think of lusts of the flesh as just sexual sins, but in Paul's mind they include much more. He mentions sexual sins, "religious" sins, interpersonal sins, and drinking sins.

sexual immorality, impurity and debauchery: These three terms cover all manner of sexual sin: public or private, between married or unmarried, natural or unnatural. Sexual sin was particularly rampant in Paul's world. In fact, "It has been said that chastity was the one completely new virtue which Christianity introduced into the pagan world."[5]

idolatry: Idolatry includes the worship of anything other than God, as well as covetousness and greed (Colossians 3:5).

witchcraft: *Pharmakeia* meant the use of drugs or potions, but in the New Testament it took on the added meaning of magic or tampering with supernatural powers.

and the like: Paul considered his list of the acts of a sinful nature to be representative but not exhaustive.

fruit: The word is singular; Paul lists nine characteristics of the one fruit.

---

1. John Rea, *The Holy Spirit in the Bible* (Lake Mary, Fla.: Creation House, 1990), p. 281.
2. F. F. Bruce, *Paul: Apostle of the Heart Set Free* (Grand Rapids, Mich.: Eerdmans, 1977), p. 21.
3. C. S. Lewis, *The Screwtape Letters* (Uhrichsville, Ohio: Barbour, 1990), p. 116.
4. R. Kent Hughes, *Colossians and Philemon: The Supremacy of Christ* (Westchester, Ill.: Crossway, 1989), p. 71. Literally, this verse is warning about being taken captive, as a prisoner. Some translations read "basic principles," but a better translation is "elemental spirits" who control false doctrine.
5. William Barclay, quoted in Leon Morris, *Galatians: Paul's Charter of Christian Freedom* (Downers Grove, Ill.: InterVarsity, 1996), p. 170.

Diversity in Unity: The Gifts of the Spirit

1 Corinthians 12:1-30

Let it be firmly said that the church cannot be fully or freely the church without the presence and operation of the gifts of the Holy Spirit. What is depicted therefore in 1 Corinthians —and recurring in our day—is in no sense a peripheral matter but is crucial to the life of the church. For the recurrence of the charismata of the Holy Spirit signals the church's recovery of its spiritual roots and its emergence in the twentieth century with fresh power and vitality.[1]

▼ ▼ ▼ ▼ ▼ ▼ ▼ ▼ ▼ ▼ ▼ ▼ ▼ ▼ ▼ ▼ ▼ ▼

Overview   10 minutes

❶ *Allow people to share about what happened in their relationships this week as they sought the Spirit's help in expressing their faith through love. Then have someone read the following aloud.*

My husband, Rich, is not known around our house as an expert handy man. But one spring, he decided to build a deck onto the back of our home. He began by marking off about a dozen spots for posts, and then started to dig two-and-a-half-foot holes by hand with a post-hole digger.

In our backyard at the time was a large tree with an enormous root system. Because of these roots, the digging was slow going. It eventually came to a complete halt. I was resigned to the fact that we'd never have a deck until Rich got the idea of renting a power auger. With this gasoline-powered machine he was able to dig through those massive roots and within just a couple hours had all the holes dug. What a difference using power tools can make!

God has given to His church gifts that are a lot like power tools. They enable Christians to do the work of the ministry more effectively and efficiently. Where the gifts of the Holy Spirit are exercised, churches are often vibrant and growing. When we rely on our own efforts and natural talents to build the church, we can accomplish some things, but building the kingdom of God becomes as much of a struggle as digging through huge roots with a post-hole digger.

I still remember a fellowship meeting where my husband felt the Lord telling him someone there was abusing drugs. My husband spoke up, saying that God knew about the problem and was calling that person to give up the drugs. After the meeting a young man came up to my husband shaking and confessed that just the night before, he had smoked marijuana. He was a leader in a nationally known campus ministry. As a result of this word, he repented and we prayed for him. This is an example of what Paul described in 1 Corinthians 14:25, "The secrets of the heart are laid bare." How much more effective this was than hours of "sermonizing" about drug abuse!

In this final session, we will look at Paul's discussion of spiritual gifts in 1 Corinthians. Our goals will be to understand what spiritual gifts are, how God intended them to function in Corinth, and how He wants them to function today.

▼ ▼ ▼ ▼ ▼ ▼ ▼ ▼ ▼ ▼ ▼ ▼ ▼ ▼ ▼ ▼ ▼ ▼

Beginning   10 minutes

1. What is one question or concern you have about the gifts of the Spirit?

▼ ▼ ▼ ▼ ▼ ▼ ▼ ▼ ▼ ▼ ▼ ▼ ▼ ▼ ▼ ▼ ▼ ▼ ▼ ▼

The Text   5 minutes

❶ *Have someone read the passage aloud. You may also want to refer to the reference notes on pages 108-110.*

Now about **spiritual gifts**, brothers, I do not want you to be ignorant. You know that when you were pagans, somehow or other you were influenced and led astray to mute idols. Therefore I tell you that no one who is **speaking by the Spirit** of God says, "Jesus be cursed," and no one can say, "**Jesus is Lord**," except by the Holy Spirit.

There are different kinds of **gifts**, but the same Spirit. There are different kinds of **service**, but the same Lord. There are different kinds of **working**, but the same God works all of them in all men.

Now to each one the manifestation of the Spirit is given for the common good. To one there is given through the Spirit the message of **wisdom,** to another the message of **knowledge** by means of the same Spirit, to another faith by the same Spirit, to another gifts of healing by that one Spirit, to another miraculous powers, to another **prophecy**, to another distinguishing between spirits, to another speaking in different kinds of tongues, and to still another the interpretation of tongues. All these are the work of one and the same Spirit, and he gives them to each one, just as he determines.

The body is a unit, though it is made up of many parts; and though all its parts are many, they form one body. **So it is with Christ.** For we were all **baptized by one Spirit** into one body—whether Jews or Greeks, slave or free—and we were all **given the one Spirit to drink**.

Now the body is not made up of one part but of many. If the foot should say, "Because I am not a hand, I do not belong to the body," it would not for that reason cease to be part of the body. And if the ear should say, "Because I am not an eye, I do not belong to the body," it would not for that reason cease to be part of the body. If the whole body were an eye, where would the sense of hearing be? If the whole body were an ear, where would the sense of smell be? But in fact God has arranged the parts in the body, every one of them, just as he wanted them to be. If they were all one part, where would the body be? As it is, there are many parts, but one body.

The eye cannot say to the hand, "I don't need you!" And the head cannot say to the feet, "I don't need you!" On the contrary, those parts of the body that seem to be **weaker** are indispensable, and the parts that we think are **less honorable** we treat with special honor. And the parts that are unpresentable are treated with special modesty, while our presentable parts need no special treatment. But God has combined the members of the body and has given greater honor to the parts that lacked it, so that there should be no division in the body, but that its parts should have equal concern for each other. If one part suffers, every part suffers with it; if one part is honored, every part rejoices with it.

Now you are the body of Christ, and each one of you is a part of it. And in the church God has appointed **first** of all apostles, **second** prophets, **third** teachers, then workers of miracles, also those having gifts of healing, those able to help others, those with gifts of administration, and those speaking in different kinds of tongues. Are all apostles? Are all prophets? Are all teachers? Do all work miracles? Do all have gifts of healing? Do all speak in tongues? Do all interpret? But **eagerly desire the greater gifts**.

(1 Corinthians 12:1-31)

▼ ▼ ▼ ▼ ▼ ▼ ▼ ▼ ▼ ▼ ▼ ▼ ▼ ▼ ▼ ▼ ▼ ▼ ▼

Understanding the Text   20 minutes

2. What problem in Corinth does Paul address in 1 Corinthians 12?

3. Ecstatic speech is common in many religions. People sing, talk, and prophesy under the influence of drugs, spirits, or self-induced trances. According to the first paragraph in the text above, how can we know whether the Holy Spirit is behind someone's speech?

4. In the second paragraph, Paul repeats the same idea three times.

   a. What does he say is different?

   b. What does he say is the same?

   c. What is Paul's point, and why do you think he feels the need to emphasize it through repetition?

5. In the third paragraph, Paul states a simple thesis, illustrates this thesis with examples, and then concludes with a summary statement.
   a. What is his thesis?

   b. What false notions about spiritual gifts might Paul be correcting with this one statement?

   c. How does Paul go on to back up his thesis with examples?

   d. Paul's summary statement is the last sentence in this paragraph. What new piece of information does he add to his argument?

   e. What false idea or sinful attitude do you think he was attempting to correct with this new information?

6. Paul really wants to drive his point home, so he comes up with a terrific analogy for how spiritual gifts are to operate in the church: the human body. What makes the physical body such a good illustration of the church in operation?

7. In paragraphs five and six, Paul personifies body parts in order to address two problems.

   a. How does he encourage those who might think they are inferior because they lack certain gifts?

   b. How does he caution those who might think they are superior?

   c. What are some examples of spiritual gifts that some people think are more valuable than other gifts?

   d. What are some examples of spiritual gifts that Christians sometimes feel the church can do without?

   e. What are some examples of spiritual gifts you feel are sorely missed in your church experience?

8. Paul tells the Corinthians to "eagerly desire the greater gifts." In chapter 14 he singles out prophecy for special mention as a desirable gift. What can we learn about spiritual gifts from the fact that it is possible—even necessary—to eagerly desire those we have not yet exercised?

▼ ▼ ▼ ▼ ▼ ▼ ▼ ▼ ▼ ▼ ▼ ▼ ▼ ▼ ▼ ▼ ▼ ▼
Applying the Text   20 minutes

9. Throughout this chapter, Paul emphasizes the importance of unity and diversity. One must not be sacrificed for the sake of the other. Yet, groups and individuals have difficulty keeping these two truths in balance. What do you think are some practical things a local body can do to both maintain unity and allow for diversity? What are some things it *shouldn't* do?

10. a. What are the implications for us of the following things Paul says about the gifts? The distribution and arrangement of gifts within the church is the sovereign work of God. (verses 11,18,28)

b. We should eagerly desire the greater gifts. (verse 31)

c. The Spirit gives the gifts for the common good. (verse 7)

It's been said that faith is spelled R-I-S-K. People of faith in the Bible took risks all the time. Abraham took a risk when he laid his only son Isaac on the altar. Moses took a risk when he led the nation of Israel to the foot of the Red Sea. Peter took a risk when he reached out to heal the lame man at the temple (session 4). They had faith that God would come through. When one Christian leader I knew exercised spiritual gifts, he said he felt like a plumber going to a job with an empty toolbox. The whole time he was trusting God to supply the right tool for the job!

11. a. How does it make you feel to know there will always be a sense of risk involved when you step out to do something for the Lord?

b. What difference does it make for you to view spiritual gifts not as something you possess, but as something for which you are totally dependent upon God?

Many believers think the gifts must suddenly appear in their lives fully mature and perfected, or they are not real spiritual gifts. (This belief is especially common regarding the more obviously supernatural gifts, such as healing.) However, in other areas of their lives, such as prayer or effectively sharing the gospel, these same people believe they are on a growth curve and that improvement will come with practice.

12. Would you approach the gifts of the Spirit any differently if you knew you were on a growth curve in exercising them? (For example, have you ever expressed a gift in an underdeveloped or immature way?)

13. a. The Corinthians were particularly impressed with the gift of tongues. Paul needed to put tongues in proper perspective for them so that they would appreciate all the manifestations of the Spirit. With which gifts are you most impressed and why?

b. Which manifestations of the Spirit do you tend to ignore? Why do you think that is?

14. The fact is that 1 Corinthians doesn't answer all the questions we might have about how the Spirit intends to gift His church today. (What is a "message of knowledge"? Does everyone have the potential to prophesy? Should "miraculous powers" be operating in our churches?)

a. What questions do you still have about spiritual gifts?

b. How can your group go about seeking answers?

15. End by letting each group member tell one or more things he or she has gained from this study of the Holy Spirit.

Assignment

Fred Astaire was a gifted dancer. His movements were always smooth and graceful, even if he was just dancing with a coat rack. He made it look so easy! Paul used the Greek word for "grace" (*charis*) as the root word for "gifts" (*charismata*). God gifts people with grace to do certain jobs in the church. Because of God's grace, they make the jobs look easy!

One way to discover your gifts is to determine how God has "graced" you. This week, take some time to reflect on yourself. What things do you do "gracefully"? (In other words, what do you make look easy?) Is it an area of service like giving or extending mercy? Is it prophecy or healing? Then find a trusted Christian friend who knows you well. Ask them for feedback on your personal reflections. Remember, once we discover those areas in which God has gifted us, Paul exhorts us to exercise our gifts to the fullest (see Romans 12:6-8).

On the other hand, Paul urges us to desire that the Spirit would gift us for the common good in ways we have not yet exercised. What opportunities for service do you think God wants you to desire?

▼ ▼ ▼ ▼ ▼ ▼ ▼ ▼ ▼ ▼ ▼ ▼ ▼ ▼ ▼ ▼ ▼ ▼ ▼
Prayer

Paul wrote that to *each one* is given the manifestation of the Spirit. Take time as a group to pray that the Spirit would have His way in both distributing and arranging gifts to each person in your group. Pray particularly for those who haven't a clue yet as to how God has gifted them. Finally, allow each person an opportunity to give thanks for ways in which he or she has grown closer to the Holy Spirit through this study.

▼ ▼ ▼ ▼ ▼ ▼ ▼ ▼ ▼ ▼ ▼ ▼ ▼ ▼ ▼ ▼ ▼ ▼ ▼
Reference Notes

Setting: In the first eleven chapters, Paul addressed a number of areas in which the Corinthian believers needed correction. He is now beginning a new subject: *pneumatikon*, "spiritual gifts," or more literally, "spiritual matters," "things of the Spirit," or even "spirituality." It is clear from the context that Corinth was not *totally* ignorant of "spiritual matters." Paul was not giving them new information, but corrective information. They were out of control and out of order, and they were particularly enamored by one gift: speaking in tongues. Paul needed to correct their mis-understandings and practices of "things of the Spirit." His desire was not to eliminate the gift of tongues, but to see it used prop-erly (chapter 14).

spiritual gifts: Paul uses two different Greek words that are both translated "spiritual gifts": *pneumatikon* (12:1) and *charis-mata* (12:4; used in the New Testament sixteen times by Paul and once by Peter). The distinction between these two words lies in their roots. *Pneuma* or "spirit" puts the emphasis in *pneumatikon* on the Holy Spirit. *Charis* or "grace" is the root of *charismata* and puts the emphasis on the manifestation of the Spirit through gifts of grace. Throughout the New Testament, *charismata* can refer to the gift of salvation, various blessings from God, or gifts that enable believers to serve God. It is clear from the language and the variation in the lists of gifts here in 1 Corinthians (12:8-10,28-30; 13:1-3,8; 14:6,26) and elsewhere in the New Testament (Romans 12:6-8) that Paul never intended for these to be exhaustive lists.

speaking by the Spirit: Verses 2-3 are difficult to interpret. It is possible, though, that Paul wants to make a sharp distinction between the Corinthians' former experiences with ecstatic utterances during pagan worship and Spirit-inspired gifts during Christian worship. One major distinction is what is confessed about the person of Jesus Christ (see 1 John 4:1-3).

Jesus is Lord: Paul means more than just the mouthing of this phrase. In the early church, these words were profoundly meaningful, acknowledging the deity of Christ, His resurrection from the dead and His supremacy over all pagan deities.

gifts . . . service . . . working: There isn't much significance to the variation in words here. All are manifestations of the Spirit. Paul is using repeated parallel sentences for emphasis.

wisdom . . . knowledge: Interpreters differ over how to define these gifts. Paul's primary concern in this passage is not to categorize and describe the individual gifts but to correct problems in the Corinthian church. One such problem was the Corinthians' misunderstanding of wisdom (1 Corinthians 1:17-2:16), and knowledge (1 Corinthians 8:1-3), which they had completely divorced from the Holy Spirit.

prophecy: Some people say prophecy is the same as teaching or preaching the Word of God. Others would argue that the Bible treats these functions very differently. For further study on this issue, see Exodus 4:15-16; 7:1; Nehemiah 8:7-8; Jeremiah 1:1-9; Acts 13:1; Romans 12:6-8; Ephesians 4:11-13; 1 Timothy 4:11-16; 2 Timothy 2:15; 3:16-17; 4:1-5.

So it is with Christ: Paul is referring here to the church, or the body of Christ, and not to the person of Christ. This is a figure of speech called *metonymy*.

baptized by one Spirit . . . given the one Spirit to drink: Note the images Paul uses: Christians are to be both *immersed in* the Spirit as well as *filled with* the Spirit.

weaker . . . less honorable: Paul seems to be alluding to the internal organs and the sexual organs respectively. His point, however, is not to have Christians try to identify which body part they are like. His point is that all parts should have equal concern for each other.

first . . . second . . . third: These words appear to rank the gifts and so to contradict Paul's point that no gift is superior to any other. However, this list, like the other in verses 8-10, is *ad hoc*. Paul is pointing out the tremendous diversity God has designed into His church. The apparent ranking of the first three may have to do with their order of appearance in the founding of the church.

eagerly desire the greater gifts: We should interpret this statement with 1 Corinthians 14:1-5. Paul views certain gifts as "greater" or more valuable than tongues because they are *intelligible* and thereby more edifying to the church. He does not intend to introduce a hierarchy of gifts. Also, while he urges the Corinthians to "eagerly desire" certain gifts, the motive for this desire is supposed to be the spreading of God's work in the world, not the status of the individual who exercises a gift.

---

1. J. Rodman Williams, *Renewal Theology: Salvation, the Holy Spirit, and Christian Living* (Grand Rapids, Mich.: Zondervan, 1990), p. 327.

Bibliography

Barton, Bruce B., Comfort, Philip W., Veerman, David R., Wilson, Neil, Life Application Bible Commentary: John, edited by Grant Osborne, (Wheaton, Ill.: Tyndale, 1993).

Bruce, F. F,. Acts, The New International Commentary on the New Testament (Grand Rapids, Mich.: Eerdmans, 1980).

Bruce, F. F., Paul: Apostle of the Heart Set Free (Grand Rapids, Mich.: Eerdmans, 1977).

Carson, D. A., The Gospel According to John, (Grand Rapids, Mich.: Eerdmans, 1991).

Cole, Alan, The Epistle of Paul to the Galatians (Grand Rapids, Mich.: Eerdmans, 1965).

Deere, Jack, Surprised by the Power of the Spirit (Grand Rapids, Mich.: Zondervan, 1993).

Fee, Gordon D., God's Empowering Presence (Peabody, Mass.: Hendrickson, 1994).

Fee, Gordon D., Paul, the Spirit, and the People of God (Peabody, Mass.: Hendrickson, 1996).

Fee, Gordon D., The First Epistle to the Corinthians (Grand Rapids, Mich.: Eerdmans, 1987).

Gaebelein, Frank E., general editor, The Expositor's Bible Commentary, Matthew, Mark & Luke, John & Acts (Grand Rapids, Mich.: Zondervan, 1984).

Geldenhuys, Norval, The Gospel of Luke (Grand Rapids, Mich.: Eerdmans, 1993).

Green, Michael, I Believe in the Holy Spirit (Grand Rapids, Mich.: Eerdmans, 1975).

Grudem, Wayne, Are Miraculous Gifts for Today? (Grand Rapids, Mich.: Zondervan, 1996).

Hendriksen, William, Exposition of the Gospel According to Luke (Grand Rapids, Mich.: Baker, 1978).

Hendriksen, William, New Testament Commentary: The Gospel of John, (Grand Rapids, Mich.: Baker Book House, 1953).

Jane Rumph, Stories from the Front Lines (Grand Rapids, Mich.: Baker, 1996).

Keener, Craig, Three Crucial Questions about the Holy Spirit (Grand Rapids, Mich.: Baker, 1996).

LaSor, William Sanford, Church Alive, (Ventura Regal Books, 1972).

Lloyd-Jones, D. Martyn, Romans: The Sons of God, Exposition of Chapter 8:5-17 (Grand Rapids, Mich.: Zondervan, 1975).

Longenecker, Richard N., Galatians (Dallas, Tex.: Word, 1990).

Mallone, George, Those Controversial Gifts (Downers Grove, Ill.: InterVarsity, 1983).

Marshall, I. Howard, The Acts of the Apostles: An Introduction
    and Commentary (Grand Rapids, Mich.: Eerdmans, 1980).
Morris, Leon, Galatians: Paul's Charter of Christian Freedom
    (Downers Grove, Ill.: InterVarsity, 1996).
Morris, Leon, The Epistle to the Romans (Grand Rapids, Mich.:
    Eerdmans, 1988).
Morris, Leon, The First Epistle of Paul to the Corinthians,
    (Grand Rapids, Mich.: Eerdmans, 1958).
Morris, Leon, The New International Commentary on the New
    Testament: The Gospel According to John, (Grand Rapids,
    Mich.: Eerdmans, 1971).
Nathan, Rich, and Wilson, Ken, Empowered Evangelicals (Ann
    Arbor, Mich.: Servant, 1995).
Rea, John, The Holy Spirit in the Bible (Lake Mary, Fla.:
    Creation House, 1990).
Ridderbos, Herman N., The Epistle of Paul to the Churches of
    Galatia (Grand Rapids, Mich.: Eerdmans, 1953).
Stibbe, Mark, Know Your Spiritual Gifts (London, England:
    Marshall Pickering, 1997).
Stott, John R .W., The Message of Galatians (Downers Grove, Ill.:
    InterVarsity, 1968).
Stott, John R. W., Romans: God's Good News for the World
    (Downers Grove, Ill.: InterVarsity, 1994).
Stott, John R. W., The Message of Acts (Leicester, England:
    InterVarsity Press, 1990).
Williams, J. Rodman, Renewal Theology: Salvation, the Holy
    Spirit, and Christian Living (Grand Rapids, Mich.:
    Zondervan, 1990).
Wimber, John, Power Evangelism (San Francisco: Harper &
    Row, 1986).